P9-DFG-548

Microsoft

Microsoft®

OneNote® 2010 Plain & Simple

Peter Weverka

Published with the authorization of Microsoft Corporation by:
O'Reilly Media, Inc.
1005 Gravenstein Highway North
Sebastopol, California 95472

ISBN: 978-0-7356-6054-0

1 2 3 4 5 6 7 8 9 TI 6 5 4 3 2 1

Printed and bound in Canada.

Microsoft Press books are available through booksellers and distributors worldwide. If you need support related to this book, email Microsoft Press Book Support at mspinput@microsoft.com. Please tell us what you think of this book at http://www.microsoft.com/learning/booksurvey.

Acquisitions and Developmental Editor: Kenyon Brown
Production Editor: Jasmine Perez
Technical Reviewer: Kristen Merritt
Copyeditor: Nancy Sixsmith
Proofreader: John Pierce
Indexer: Seth Maislin
Cover Design: Karen Montgomery
Illustrator: Rob Romano

For Dolly Schiller

Contents

Introduction: About This Book 1

What's New in Microsoft OneNote 2010 5

What do you think of this book? We want to hear from you!

Microsoft is interested in hearing your feedback so we can continually improve our books and learning resources for you. To participate in a brief online survey, please visit:

www.microsoft.com/learning/booksurvey/

Getting Started with OneNote 2010   15

Storing Your Notes   27

Writing Basic Notes   43

Taking Notes to Another Level — 57

Putting a Table in a Note — 75

Linking Your Notes — 83

Making OneNote Easier to Use — 95

Spell Checking Your Notes

Drawing Notes

Organizing Your Notes

Searching for Stray Notes 145

Housecleaning in OneNote 153

Conducting Research in OneNote 2010 163

Distributing Your Notes 173

Using OneNote with Other Office 2010 Applications 181

Sharing Notebooks with Others 191

Customizing OneNote 2010 199

Using OneNote Web App 215

Acknowledgments

Thanks to Ken Brown of O'Reilly Media for giving me the opportunity to write this book and for his many suggestions for making it better. I also want to thank technical editor Kristen Merritt for making sure all instructions are accurate, copy editor Nancy Sixsmith for going over the text so carefully, and the O'Reilly team for their excellent layout work.

1

Introduction: About This Book

Microsoft OneNote 2010 Plain & Simple is for users of Microsoft OneNote 2010 who want to make the most of the program and learn how to do tasks quickly. Don't look in this book to find out how OneNote 2010 works. Look in this book to find out how you can get your work done faster and better with OneNote.

You can use this book as a tutorial or a reference. Read it one section at a time to become an expert on OneNote or keep it by your computer to refer to it when you need help. This book was written and designed so you can get the information you need and complete tasks right away.

No Computerese!

This book scrupulously avoids computerese, computerspeak, and nerd-talk. You will not scratch your head or grimace over computer jargon as you read this book.

For each task, you get a quick overview and the background information you need to proceed wisely. Then you plunge right in. You get concise, step-by-step instructions for completing the task. And each set of instructions is accompanied by screenshots that show you precisely how to do the task and where to do it in OneNote.

Occasionally, you encounter a See Also element that refers you to a task similar to the one being described. You also find Tips that offer shortcuts and other useful advice. When you need to tread softly or carefully, you find a Caution element explaining why caution is the order of the day.

A Comprehensive Approach

Microsoft OneNote 2010 Plain & Simple is comprehensive. It covers every nook and cranny of OneNote.

When I describe how to do a task, I start by describing what I think is the easiest, fastest way. Then I tell you all the other ways to do it as well.

You are invited to explore all the commands in OneNote as you read this book. Everything is covered here.

A Quick Overview

This book is your guide to getting the most from OneNote. It's jam-packed with how-tos, advice, shortcuts, and tips. Here is a bare outline of what you'll find in this book:

Section 2 describes what's new in OneNote 2010. Go there if you're familiar with the previous version of OneNote and you want to get acquainted with the new stuff.

Sections 3 and 4 get you up and running. They explain the basics of creating and opening notebooks; navigating; and creating the sections, section groups, pages, and page groups you need to organize and store notes.

Section 5 explains the nitty-gritty of OneNote: How to write a note, format text on a note, move and copy text, and create bulleted and numbered lists.

Section 6 describes advanced note-taking, including how to write outlines, put pictures and screen clippings in notes, attach a file and file printout to a note, write math equations, and take audio and video notes. You also find out how to jot down a side note and place it later on into a notebook.

Section 7 explains all you need to know about formatting and laying out tables.

Section 8 is all about linking. It explores how to create links between different notebooks, sections, and pages; how to hyperlink to web pages and files; and how to take linked notes.

Section 9 describes all the things you can do to make working with OneNote easier, including how to minimize the ribbon, navigation bar, and page tabs; how to dock OneNote; and how to change screen views.

Section 10 takes on spell-checking.

Section 11 explains how to draw notes with lines, freeform lines, and shapes.

Section 12 describes tagging and other ways to organize notes, and Section 13 explores how to search for stray notes.

Section 14 explains housecleaning chores, including how to delete and restore sections and pages and how to back up a notebook.

Section 15 shows how to use the Research task pane to research topics and translate text.

Section 16 looks at distributing notes by printing and e-mailing them, and how to save OneNote pages, sections, and notebooks in alternate file formats.

Section 17 explores how to use OneNote and Microsoft Outlook 2010 to handle tasks, calendar events, meetings, and contact information.

Section 18 describes how to share notebooks and how to find and read notes written by your coauthors.

Section 19 delves into OneNote Web App, the online version of OneNote, and shows how you can use it to collaborate with others when taking notes.

Section 20 explains how to customize the ribbon and the Quick Access toolbar to become a more efficient user of OneNote.

A Few Assumptions

Pardon me, but I made a few assumptions about you, the reader of this book.

I assumed that you are experienced enough with computers to know how the basics: how to turn the thing on, and what "click" and what "double-click" mean, for example. I assumed that Microsoft Office 2010 (OneNote is part of the Office 2010 suite) is already installed on your computer.

What's New in OneNote 2010

The biggest difference between OneNote 2010 and previous versions of the application is the screen itself. OneNote, like the other applications in the Office suite, now offers the ribbon and the Quick Access toolbar. What's more, where the Office button used to be on the left side of the ribbon, there is now the File tab. Click this tab to visit Microsoft Backstage and take care of saving files, opening files, and doing other file-management tasks.

> **See Also**
>
> "What's New in Microsoft OneNote 2010" (Section 2) on page 5 for a complete look at all the new features.

A Final Word

I hope you find this book helpful. When I wrote it, I had these goals on mind:

- To provide clear instructions for completing OneNote tasks
- To steer you to things you can do in OneNote that you didn't know you could do
- To make you a confident OneNote user

Good luck in your adventures with OneNote!

2

What's New in Microsoft OneNote 2010

With the addition of the ribbon and Quick Access toolbar, Microsoft OneNote 2010 looks much like the other Microsoft Office 2010 applications. The ribbon and Quick Access toolbar work the same way in OneNote as they do in Microsoft Word 2010, Microsoft Excel 2010, and Microsoft PowerPoint 2010, for example.

Unlike its predecessors, OneNote 2010 offers a Styles gallery for quickly formatting text and gives you the ability to create links between notebooks, sections, and pages so you can jump from place to place quickly. You can also dock OneNote to the side of the screen, which makes it easier to take notes from a Word document or web page.

To retrieve an older version of a page, you can summon it with the Page Versions command. You can use the Mini Translator to translate a word or phrase. You can formulate complex math equations without having to import them from elsewhere.

OneNote and Outlook now work hand in hand. Transferring data from Outlook to OneNote is only a matter of clicking the OneNote button in Outlook.

Using the Ribbon

The *ribbon* is the assortment of tabs, buttons, and commands that appear along the top of the OneNote screen.

Click a tab name on the ribbon to open a different tab and be able to use its buttons and commands. There are seven tabs in all: File, Home, Insert, Share, Draw, Review, and View. Each tab provides buttons and commands for doing similar tasks.

Within each tab, buttons and commands are divided into *groups*. You can see the group names along the bottom of the

ribbon. These group names help you understand what buttons and commands do.

Besides the standard tabs, OneNote sometimes presents a *contextual tab*. Contextual tabs appear on the ribbon only when you need them. For example, when you work on a table, the Table Tools Layout tab appears; it offers commands for working with tables. Look for contextual tabs to the right of the standard tabs on the ribbon.

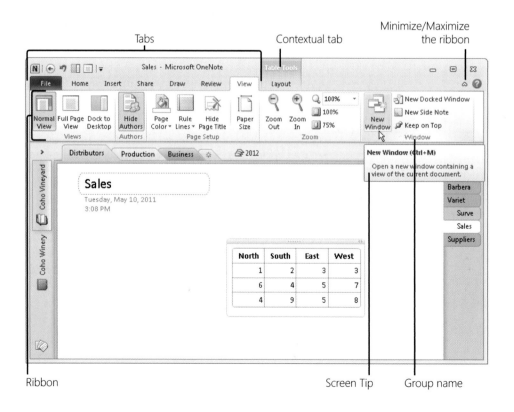

You can click the Minimize/Maximize the ribbon button (or press Ctrl+F1) to hide and display the ribbon. Hide the ribbon when you need more room for reading and writing notes.

Clicking the File tab, the leftmost tab on the ribbon, takes you to a special place: Microsoft Office Backstage. This is where you go to open, create, share, send, and print notebooks. Clicking Options on Microsoft Office Backstage opens the OneNote Options dialog box, in which you choose settings to make OneNote work your way.

Tip

Move the pointer over a button or command on the ribbon and you see a ScreenTip that briefly describes what the button or command does. If a shortcut key (for example, Ctrl+B) is available for activating a command, the shortcut key appears in the ScreenTip.

See Also

"Minimizing and Expanding the Ribbon" on page 98 to learn all the different ways to hide and display the ribbon.

File tab

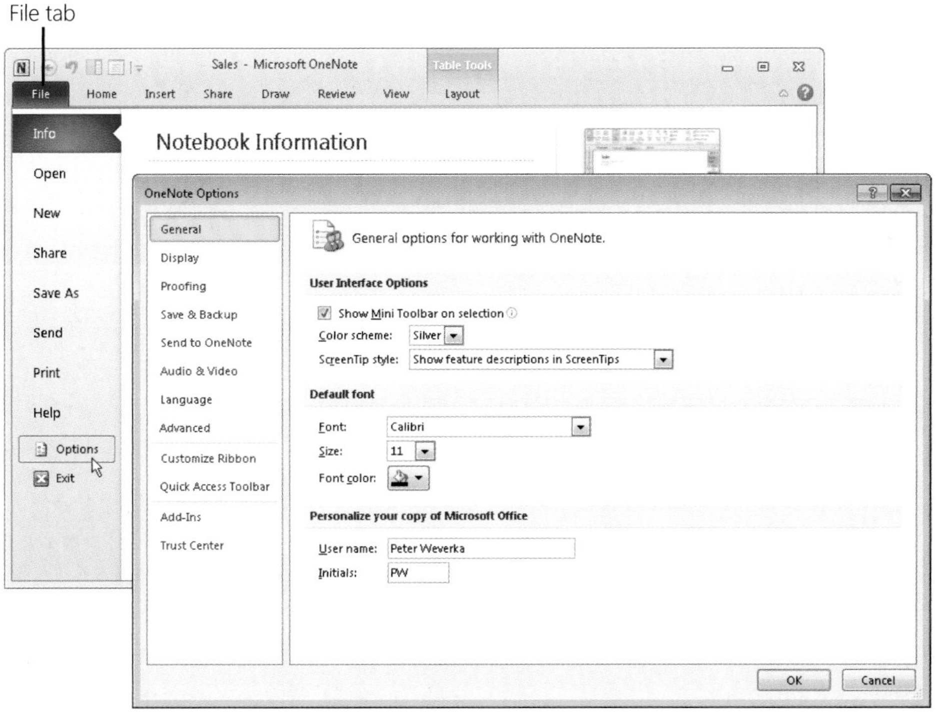

Using the Quick Access Toolbar

Above the ribbon, in the upper-left corner of the screen, is the Quick Access toolbar. This toolbar offers four convenient buttons: Back, Undo, Dock to Desktop, and Full Page View.

What's more, you can add and remove buttons from the Quick Access toolbar. You can even place the Quick Access toolbar below the ribbon.

Quick Access toolbar

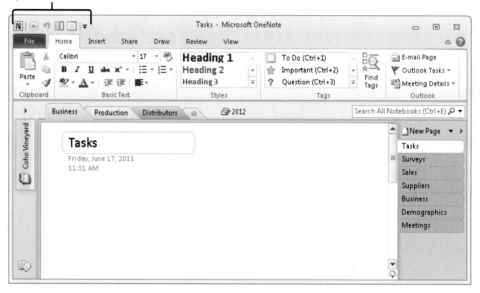

See Also

"Customizing the Quick Access Toolbar" on page 200 to learn how to add buttons, remove buttons, and move the Quick Access toolbar below the ribbon.

Formatting Text with the Styles Gallery

On the Home tab, the Styles gallery makes it easy to format text. Click a paragraph and choose a style from the gallery to instantly format all the text in the paragraph. The Styles gallery offers heading styles, as well as styles for normal text, page titles, citations, and quotes.

To apply a style, choose a style from the Styles gallery on the Home tab (or press a keyboard shortcut).

Styles gallery

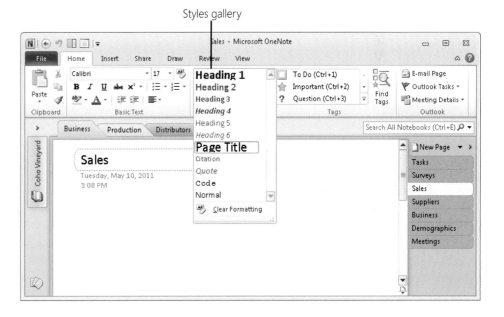

See Also

"Applying Styles to Text" on page 54 to learn all about styles and the Styles gallery.

Linking to Other Notebooks, Sections, and Pages

Linking notebooks, sections, and pages is a great way to go quickly from place to place. After you create the link, all you have to do to go to a different notebook, section, or page is click the link. The notebook, section, or page opens automatically. And to return to your original location, you can simply click the Back button on the Quick Access toolbar.

Use these techniques to create a link:

- On the Insert tab, click the Link button (or press Ctrl+K). In the Link dialog box that appears, select the link destination.

- Right-click a notebook, section, or page name and choose the Copy Link To command on the shortcut menu. Then right-click where you want the link to be and choose a Paste command.

- Type **[[page name]]** to link to a page in the currently open notebook.

See Also

"Linking to Other Places in OneNote" on page 84 to learn the ins and outs of linking notebooks, sections, and pages.

Link button

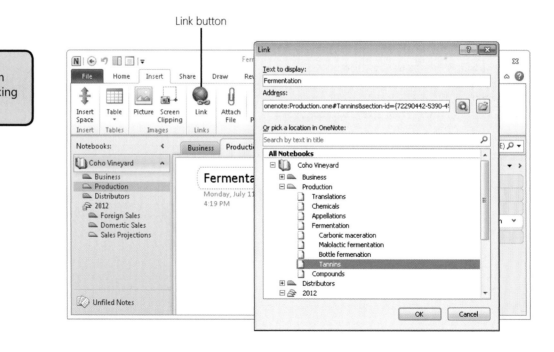

Docking OneNote on the Side of the Screen

On the Quick Access toolbar and View tab, you can click the Dock to Desktop button (or press Ctrl+Alt+D) to move the OneNote window to the side of your computer screen. With OneNote out of the way, you can take and read notes while viewing a Word document or web page. To undock OneNote, click the Dock to Desktop button a second time.

Dock to Desktop button

See Also

"Docking OneNote to the Desktop" on page 102 to learn all the details of docking the OneNote window to the desktop.

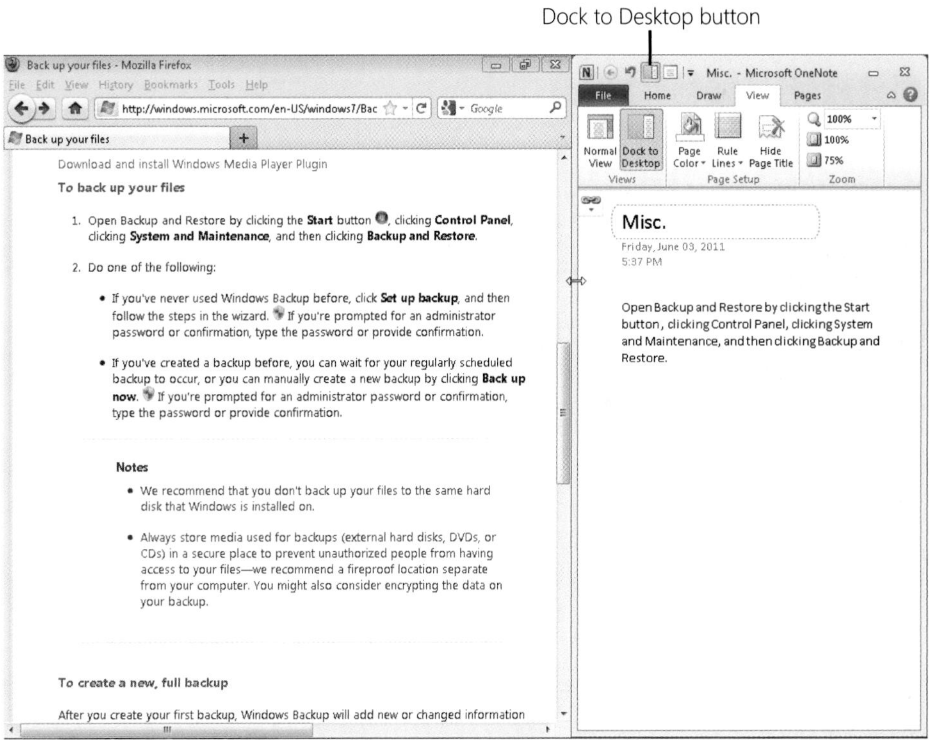

Reviewing and Restoring Page Versions

OneNote keeps backup copies of pages. To see an older version of a page, go to the Share tab and click the Page Versions button. Dated page tabs appear alongside the other page tabs. By clicking a dated page tab, you can revisit an earlier version of a page. You can also restore an earlier version of a page.

Page Versions button

See Also

"Revisiting and Restoring a Different Version of a Page" on page 37 to learn about page versions.

Sending Outlook Data to OneNote

In the Outlook 2010 Mail, Calendar, Contacts, and Tasks folders, you can find a button called OneNote. By clicking this button, you can transfer an email message, appointment, contact, or task from Outlook to a note in the OneNote application. And when you copy a meeting, contact, or task, OneNote places a link in the note that you can click to return to Outlook.

After you click the OneNote button, the Select Location in OneNote dialog box appears. Use this dialog box to copy the email message, meeting, contact, or task information to OneNote.

See Also

"Entering Outlook Information (Email, Meeting, Contact, Task) on a Page" on page 187 to learn how to transfer information from Outlook.

OneNote button

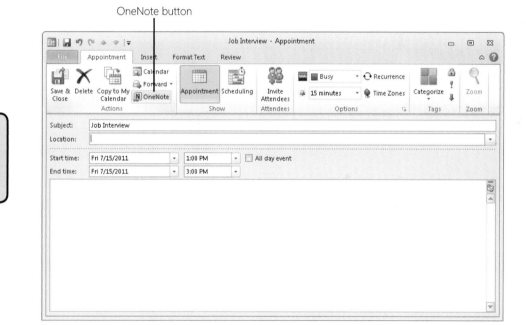

Using the Mini Translator

Use the Mini Translator to quickly translate a word or phrase. After selecting the text you want to translate, move the pointer over the text, and then move the pointer onto the Microsoft Translator toolbar to read the translation.

Microsoft Translator toolbar

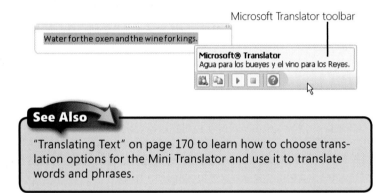

See Also

"Translating Text" on page 170 to learn how to choose translation options for the Mini Translator and use it to translate words and phrases.

Formulating and Drawing Math Equations

Use the Equation Tools Design tab to construct math equations. To open this tab, go to the Insert tab and click the Equation button (or press Alt+=). Then use the Basic Math gallery and structures to formulate an equation.

OneNote also offers the Ink to Math button on the Draw tab. After clicking this button, the Insert Ink Equation dialog box opens, in which you can draw an equation.

See Also

"Constructing Math Equations" on page 70 to learn how to write and draw math equations.

Equation Tools Design tab

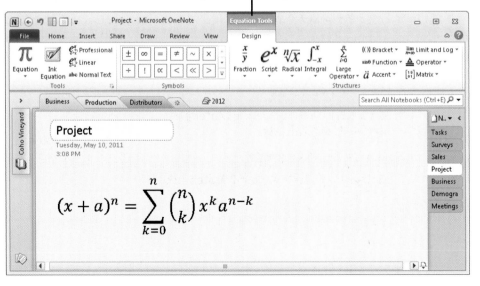

$$(x + a)^n = \sum_{k=0}^{n} \binom{n}{k} x^k a^{n-k}$$

3

Getting Started with OneNote 2010

Your first task in Microsoft OneNote 2010 is to create a notebook for storing the notes you write. After you create a notebook, you can create sections for storing the pages where notes are written, and pages for storing notes.

In OneNote 2010, notes are stored in a notebook-section-pages hierarchy that is designed to help you categorize information, write notes, and retrieve notes. You can rename notebooks, and on the Navigation bar where notebook names are listed, you can collapse and expand notebooks to hide or display their sections.

Navigating in OneNote is a matter of using the Navigation bar, section tabs, and page tabs to go from place to place.

If you used Microsoft OneNote 2007, be sure to convert your 2007 notebooks to 2010 notebooks. OneNote offers a special command for doing that.

What's Where in OneNote 2010

The purpose of OneNote is to make it easier for you to record, store, organize, and find notes. To that end, the OneNote screen is divided into these areas:

- Navigation bar: Lists the names of open notebooks, and below each note-book name, the names of its sections and section groups. Click a section name to open a different section in any open notebook.

- Section tabs: Provides one tab for each section and section group in the notebook you are currently viewing. Click a tab to go to a different section.

- Page: Shows the currently open page and notes on this page.

- Page tabs: Lists the names of pages and subpages in the currently open section. Pages are stored in sections. Click a page name to open a different page.

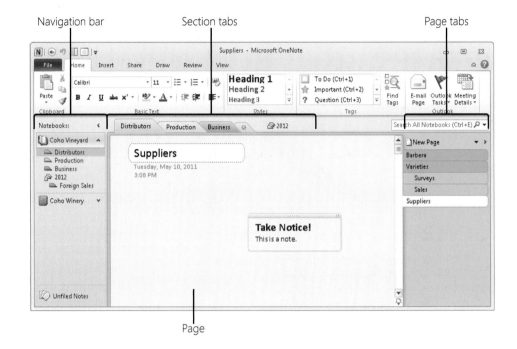

Navigation bar   Section tabs   Page tabs

Page

Try This!

Select a section name on the Navigation bar and notice that a new section opens. Then select a section name in the section tabs. You can open a different section by clicking a section name on the Navigation bar or the section tabs.

See Also

"Using the Ribbon" on page 6 to learn what the ribbon is and how to use it in OneNote.

See Also

"Handling the Navigation Bar and Page Tabs" on page 96 to learn how to expand and collapse the Navigation bar and page tabs.

Taking Advantage of the Notebook-Section-Pages Hierarchy

In OneNote, notes are stored in a notebook-section-pages hierarchy, with the foremost unit of storage being the notebook. Within each notebook, you create sections, and within sections, pages.

How you organize information in this hierarchy is important not only for retrieving information but also for conceptualizing it. In a class, for example, you can create one notebook for the class, one section for each lecture, and within each section, a page for each subject in the lecture. When the time comes to study for the final examination, you will know where to retrieve information about each subject, and moreover, your notebook-sections-pages structure will help you get a sense of how the subjects fit together.

The goal is to create notebooks, sections, and pages so that information is stored in a meaningful fashion that makes retrieving information easier. As part of that goal, think of descriptive names for your notebooks, sections, and pages when you create them.

From largest to smallest, OneNote offers these units for storing notes:

- Notebook: The file where all information is stored. The names of open notebooks appear on the Navigation bar.

- Section: A subcategory of a notebook, used to store pages. The names of sections appear on the Navigation bar below notebook names, and in the section tabs.

- Section groups: A means of organizing sections. You can store sections in a section group and in so doing be able to find and manage them more easily. After you select a section group in the section tabs, only the sections in the group appear in the section tabs.

- Page and subpage: The place where notes are recorded. Pages and subpages are stored in sections. The names of pages and subpages in the currently open section appear on the page tabs on the right side of the screen; names on subpage tabs are indented.

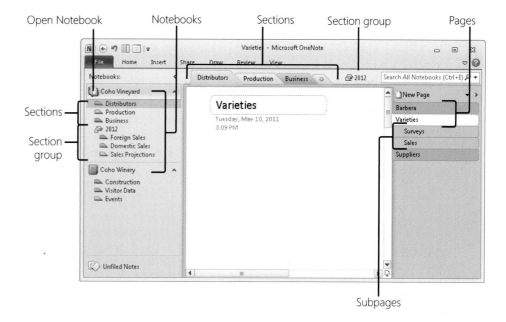

Creating a Notebook

OneNote is unusual in that you choose a folder for storing a notebook when you create it. In most applications, you create the file first and then choose a storage folder when you save the file for the first time. In OneNote, however, there isn't a Save button or Save command. Notes are saved as soon as you write them.

The first time you start OneNote, the application bids you to create a sample notebook called Personal. After that, when you open OneNote, the previous notebook you were working on opens.

To create a notebook, click the File tab and choose New to open the New Notebook window. In this window, select

Network (to store the notebook on a network or SharePoint site) or My Computer (to store the notebook on your computer). Then enter a name for your notebook, choose a folder for storing it, and click the Create Notebook button.

The name you entered for your notebook in the New Notebook window appears on the Navigation bar.

On your computer or network, OneNote creates a new folder when you create a notebook. This folder is named after the notebook itself. For example, if you named the notebook "Research," the folder is named "Research." Sections you create for your notebook are stored in the folder in the form of One-Note section files.

Create a Notebook

1. Click the File tab.
2. Click New.
3. Choose My Computer to store your notebook on a local computer, or choose Network to store it on a network.
4. Enter a descriptive name for your notebook.
5. Click Browse.
6. In the Select Folder dialog box, choose a folder for storing your notebook and click Select.
7. Click Create Notebook.

> **Tip**
>
> To go directly to the New Notebook window, right-click the Navigation bar and choose New Notebook.

> **Caution**
>
> OneNote creates a section and page for a notebook when you create it. The section is called "New Section 1," and the page is called "Untitled Page." Be sure to enter names of your own for the section and page in your new notebook.

① ② ③ ④ ⑤ ⑥ ⑦

Varieties - Microsoft OneNote

File   Home   Insert   Share   Draw   Review   View

Info

Open

New

Share

Save As

Send

Print

Help

Options

Exit

New Notebook

1. Store Notebook On:

Web
Access from any computer or browser.
Share with others (optional).

Network
Shared with others on the network or SharePoint.

My Computer

2. Name:

Trey Research

3. Location:

C:\OneNote Plain and Simple   Browse

Create
Notebook

Select Folder

‹‹ My Documents ▸ OneNote Notebooks ▸   Search OneNote Notebooks

Organize ▼   New folder

▲ 📚 Libraries   📁 Personal
  ▲ 📄 Documents
    ▲ 📁 My Documents
      📁 iframe title_files
      📁 My Data Sources
      📁 OneNote Notebooks
      📁 Outlook Files
      📁 Quicken
      📁 Public Documents
  ▷ 🎵 Music
  ▷ 🖼 Pictures
  ▷ 🎬 Videos

Folder name: OneNote Notebooks

Tools ▼   Select   Cancel

Try This!

Look for a Save button in OneNote. You won't find it! OneNote saves data as soon as you enter it, and you don't have to click a Save button.

Renaming a Notebook

Rename a notebook if the original name no longer serves your purposes. Changing the name of a notebook is just a matter of right-clicking its name on the Navigation bar, choosing Rename, and entering a new name.

Rename a Notebook

1. In the Navigation bar, right-click the name of the notebook you want to rename.

2. Choose Rename on the shortcut menu.

3. Enter a name in the Display Name text box.

4. Click OK.

Caution

Renaming a notebook does not rename the folder in which it is stored. Instead, the folder retains the original name of the notebook. This name retention can be confusing if you want to open a notebook in the Open Notebook dialog box, My Computer, or Explorer, in which your notebook's folder is listed under the notebook's original name, not the new name you gave your notebook.

Opening a Notebook

You can open more than one notebook. The names of open notebooks appear on the Navigation bar.

To open a notebook, start by clicking File and choosing Open to display the Open Notebook window. In this window, OneNote keeps a record of the previous 16 notebooks you opened. How you open a notebook depends on whether it is listed in the Open Notebook window:

- If the notebook is listed, double-click its name.

- If the notebook isn't listed, click the Open Notebook button. In the Open Notebook dialog box, select the folder where the notebook is kept, and click Open to open this folder. Then select the Open Notebook file and click Open.

Open a Notebook

1. Click File.

2. Click Open.

3. Look for your notebook in the Recently Closed Notebooks list (if its name is there, you can open the notebook by double-clicking its name).

4. Click the Open Notebook button.

5. In the Open Notebook dialog box, locate the folder named for the notebook you want to open, select the folder, and click the Open button to open the folder.

6. Select the Open Notebook file.

7. Click the Open button.

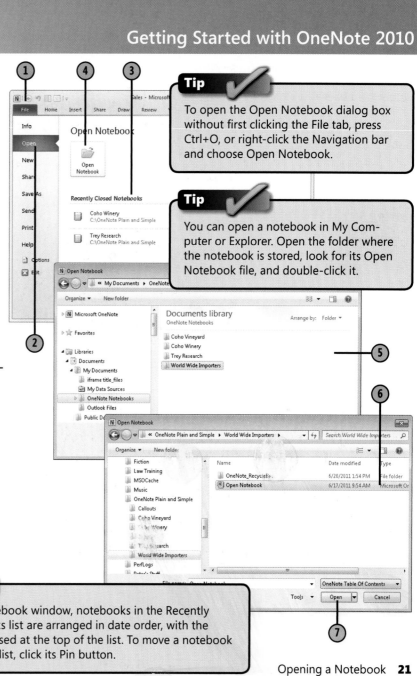

Tip
To open the Open Notebook dialog box without first clicking the File tab, press Ctrl+O, or right-click the Navigation bar and choose Open Notebook.

Tip
You can open a notebook in My Computer or Explorer. Open the folder where the notebook is stored, look for its Open Notebook file, and double-click it.

Tip
In the Open Notebook window, notebooks in the Recently Closed Notebooks list are arranged in date order, with the most recently closed at the top of the list. To move a notebook to the top of the list, click its Pin button.

Closing a Notebook

OneNote makes it pretty easy to close a notebook. All you have to do is right-click its name on the Navigation bar and choose Close This Notebook on the shortcut menu.

Close a Notebook

1. On the Navigation bar, right-click the name of the notebook you want to close.

2. Choose Close This Notebook.

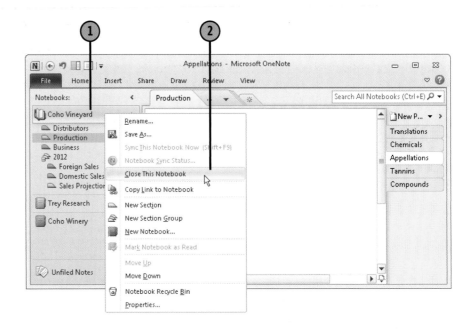

See Also

"Collapsing and Expanding Notebooks on the Navigation Bar" on page 23 to learn how to hide and display a notebook's sections on the Navigation bar.

Collapsing and Expanding Notebooks on the Navigation Bar

To keep the Navigation bar from getting too crowded, you can collapse a notebook. When a notebook is collapsed, its section names don't appear on the Navigation bar. When it is expanded, its section names appear.

To collapse or expand a notebook, click its Collapse/Expand button. This button is located to the right of notebook names on the Navigation bar.

Collapse and Expand a Notebook

① Click the Collapse button next to a notebook name.

② Click the Expand button.

Tip ✓

You can reorder notebook names on the Navigation bar. To do so, drag a name higher or lower on the list, or right-click a name and choose Move Up or Move Down.

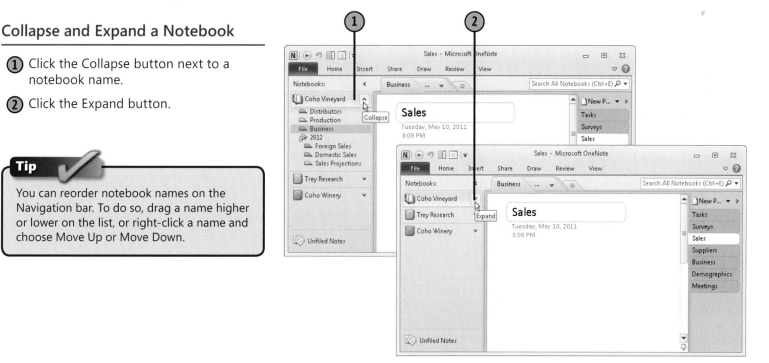

Navigating in OneNote

Getting from place to place in OneNote is a matter of using the Navigation bar, section tabs, and page tabs:

- Switching between notebooks: On the Navigation bar, click a notebook's name to switch to a different notebook. You can tell which notebook you're currently viewing because its icon shows an open notebook.

- Switching between sections: In the Navigation bar or section tabs, click a section name.

- Switching to a section in a section group: In the section tabs, click the section group name to display tabs for the section group. Then click a section tab. To return to the parent sections, click a section in the Navigation bar or click the Navigate to Parent Section Group button (this button is located to the left of the section tabs).

- Switching between pages: Click a page name in the page tabs.

See Also

Section 8, "Linking Your Notes," on page 83 to learn to create links you can click to quickly go to different sections and pages.

OneNote offers these keyboard shortcuts for navigating:

To go to	Press
The next or previous page in the section	Ctrl+PageDown; Ctrl+PageUp
The first or last page in the section	Alt+Home; Alt+End
The next or previous page you visited	Alt+Right Arrow; Alt+Left Arrow
The next or previous section	Ctrl+Tab; Ctrl+Shift+Tab

Navigate in OneNote

1. Click a notebook name on the Navigation bar to switch to a different notebook.

2. In the Navigation bar, click a section name to switch to a different section.

3. In the section tabs, click a section name to switch to a different section.

4. Click a section group name to see tabs in the section group.

5. Click a page in the page tabs to switch to a different page.

6. Click the Navigate to Parent Section Group button to return to the parent sections in the notebook.

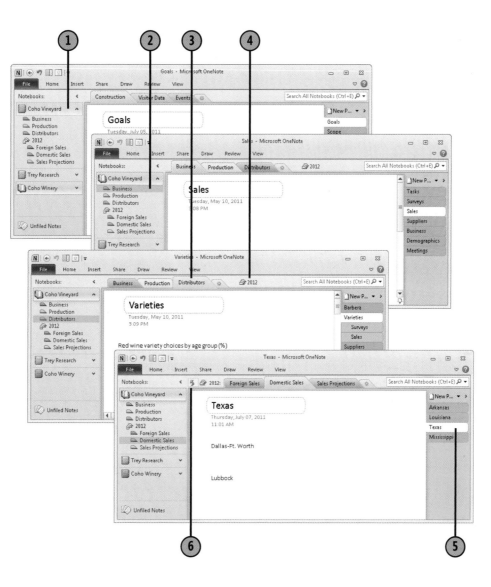

Converting OneNote 2007 Notebooks to 2010

Convert Microsoft OneNote 2007 notebooks to Microsoft OneNote 2010 to take advantage of the features not available in the 2007 edition. For example, you must convert to OneNote 2010 to share notebooks with the OneNote Web App.

To make the conversion, right-click the notebook's icon in the Navigation bar and choose Properties. Then, in the Notebook Properties dialog box, click the Convert to 2010 button.

Convert a OneNote 2007 Notebook to 2010

①　In the Navigation bar, right-click the notebook you want to convert to OneNote 2010.

②　Choose Properties on the shortcut menu.

③　Click the Convert to 2010 button.

④　In the Warning message box, click OK.

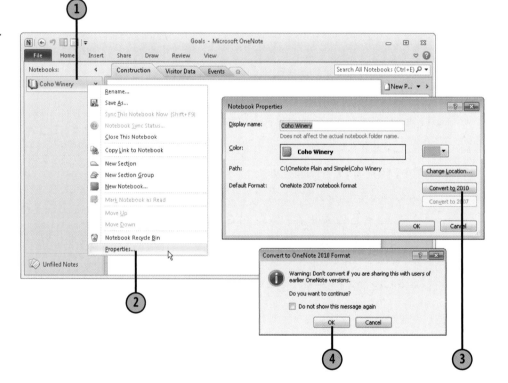

4

Storing Your Notes

Store notes in sections, section groups, pages, and page groups. The names of sections and section groups appear on the Navigation bar and in the section tabs. The names of pages and subpages that make up page groups appear on the page tabs. By thoughtfully building a scheme for storing notes in sections, section groups, pages, and page groups, you can organize information meaningfully and always be able to retrieve information.

OneNote keeps earlier versions of pages on hand in case you want to revisit or restore an older version of a page.

If keeping notes private is important to you, you can password-protect a section so that only people with the password can see a section's notes.

Creating Sections

Within a notebook, create a section for each topic you want to address. Use these techniques to create a section:

- Click the Create a New Section button (located to the right of the section tabs).

- Press Ctrl+T.

- Right-click a section or notebook name and choose New Section.

After you create a section, enter a name for it on the section tab. When you create a new section, OneNote creates the first page in the section automatically.

Create a Section

(1) Click the Create a New Section button (or press Ctrl+T).

(2) Enter a name for the section and press Enter.

(3) Enter a page name.

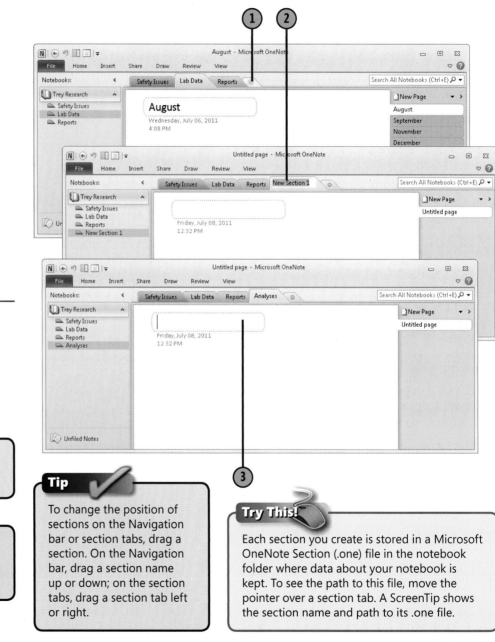

Tip

To rename a section, double-click its name in the section tab and type a new name.

See Also

"Moving, Copying, and Merging Pages and Sections" on page 132 to learn how to move or copy a section to a different notebook.

Tip

To change the position of sections on the Navigation bar or section tabs, drag a section. On the Navigation bar, drag a section name up or down; on the section tabs, drag a section tab left or right.

Try This!

Each section you create is stored in a Microsoft OneNote Section (.one) file in the notebook folder where data about your notebook is kept. To see the path to this file, move the pointer over a section tab. A ScreenTip shows the section name and path to its .one file.

Creating Section Groups

Think of a section group as a subfolder for storing sections. In the Navigation bar and section tabs, section groups always appear after sections. Place sections in a section group to organize sections better.

To create a section group, right-click a section tab or section in the Navigation bar and choose New Section Group. Then enter a name for the group.

After you create a section group, you can create sections for it or move sections into it.

On the Navigation bar and section tabs, section group names are marked with the section group icon, some stacked folders.

To open a section group, click its name on the Navigation bar or section tabs. After you open a section group, you see only section tabs belonging to the group in the section tabs area. Use these techniques to see all the sections in the notebook rather than the sections in a group:

- Click the Navigate to Parent Section Group button (located to the left of the section group name in the section tabs).
- Click a parent section in the Navigation bar.

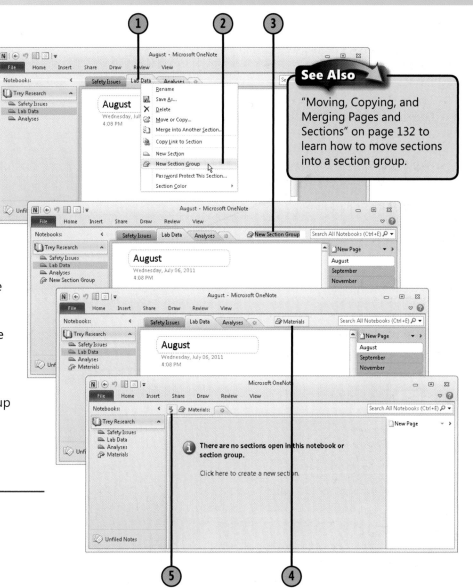

See Also

"Moving, Copying, and Merging Pages and Sections" on page 132 to learn how to move sections into a section group.

Create a Section Group

1. Right-click a tab.
2. Choose New Section Group on the shortcut menu.
3. Enter a name and press Enter.
4. Select the section group tab.
5. Click Navigate to Parent Section Group.

Creating Pages

Notes are written and kept on pages. The name of the page that is currently open appears in the title bar at the top of the OneNote screen, at the top of the page itself, and in the page tabs. Each page also lists the date and time it was created.

OneNote offers these techniques to create a page:

- Click the New Page button (or press Ctrl+N) to create a new page at the end of the currently open section. The New Page button is located at the top of the page tabs.

- In the page tabs, right-click the page you want the new page to go after, and choose New Page.

- Open the New Page gallery and choose a template, or select Page Templates to open the Templates task pane and choose a template there.

Create a Page

① Click the New Page button.

② Enter a name in the page title box.

See Also

"Creating Subpages for Page Groups" on page 34 to learn how to create subpages.

See Also

"Moving, Copying, and Merging Pages and Sections" on page 132 to learn how to move or copy all or some of the pages in a section to a different section.

After you create a page, enter its name in the page title box. You can change a page's name at any time by changing the name in the page title box.

To reorder pages in a section, select a page in the pages tab and drag it up or down.

You can create your own page templates as well as use the templates that come with OneNote. In the Templates task pane, templates you create are in the My Templates category.

Pages you create with the New Page command are made with the Default – Blank template. However, you can choose a different template as the default for pages in each section.

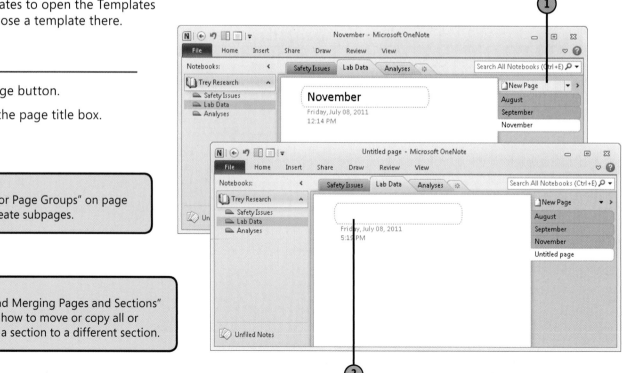

Create a Page from a Template

① Open the gallery on the New Page button.

② Notice the templates on the gallery (you can choose a template here to create a page).

③ Choose Page Templates.

④ In the Templates task pane, click an Expand button to view the templates in a category.

⑤ Click a template name and glance at the new page to see whether you like the template (you can choose a different template if you don't like the one you choose).

⑥ Click the Close button to close the task pane.

Create a Page Template

1. Create a page serving as the model for the template with text, font, page color, and other specifications.

2. Open the gallery on the New Page button.

3. Choose Page Templates.

4. In the Templates task pane, click Save Current Page as a Template.

5. In the Save As Template dialog box, enter a name for the template.

6. Click Save.

7. Click Close to close the Templates task pane.

Try This!

Create a new page with the template you created. Open the gallery on the New Page button and choose Page Templates. In the Templates task pane, open the My Templates category and click your template's name.

Choose the Default Page Template for Section Pages

(1) Open the gallery on the New Page button.

(2) Choose Page Templates.

(3) In the Templates task pane, open the Choose Default Template menu and select a template.

(4) Click the Close button to close the Templates task pane.

Tip

The page template that OneNote uses is called Default – Blank. To go back to using this template, choose it in the Templates task pane.

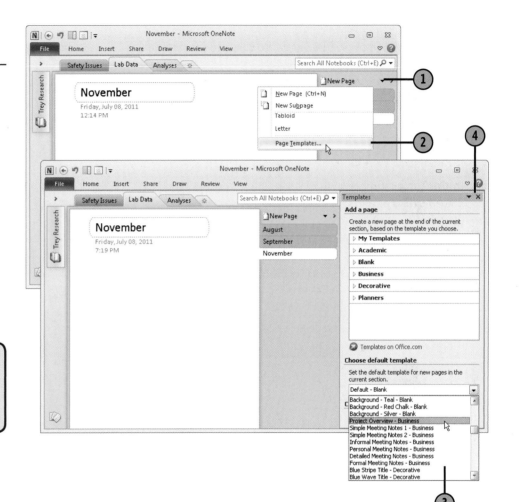

Creating Subpages for Page Groups

A page and its subpages are called a *page group*. Create subpages to store information that is subordinate to information on a page.

You can collapse the subpages in a page group. After collapsing a page group, you can easily move or copy all the pages in the group with the Move or Copy command or by dragging.

Use these techniques to create subpages for a page group:

- Create a new subpage: Open the gallery on the New Page button and choose New Subpage (or press Ctrl+Shift+Alt+N).

- Turn a page into a subpage: Right-click the page's tab and choose Make Subpage (or press Ctrl+Alt+]).

- Turn a subpage into a page: Right-click the subpage's tab and choose Promote Subpage (or press Ctrl+Alt+[).

On the page tabs, the names of subpages are indented. When you move the pointer over the first page tab in a page group, the Collapse/Expand button appears on the page tab. Use these techniques to collapse (hide) or expand (display) subpage tabs:

- Click the Collapse/Expand button on the first page tab in the page group.

- Right-click any page tab in the group, and choose Collapse Subpages or Expand Subpages.

- Press Ctrl+Shift+*.

Create a Subpage

1. Open the drop-down list on the New Page button.

2. Choose New Subpage.

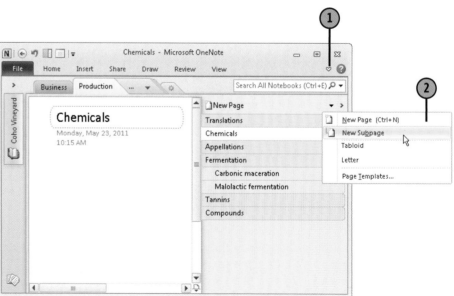

③ Drag the subpage from the bottom of the page tabs higher in the tabs.

④ Enter a title for the subpage.

⑤ Right-click a page in the page tabs

⑥ Choose Make Subpage.

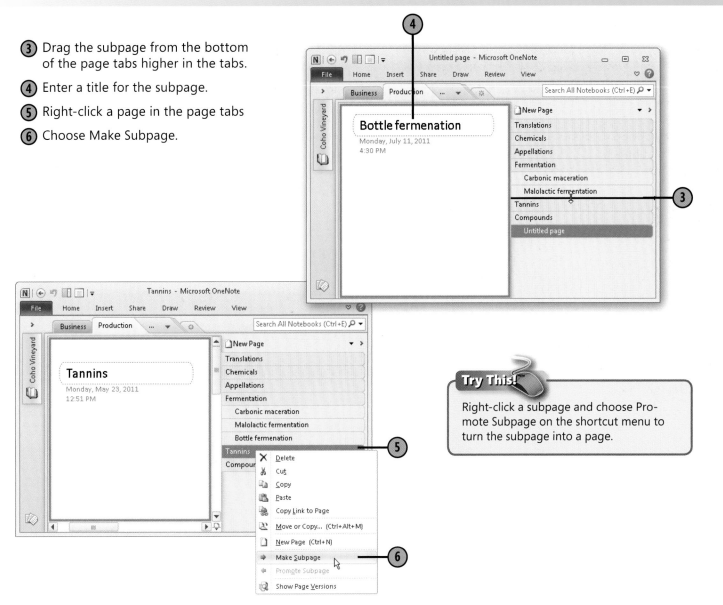

Try This!

Right-click a subpage and choose Promote Subpage on the shortcut menu to turn the subpage into a page.

Collapse and Expand Page Groups

① Click the Collapse button on the first page of a page group to hide the subpages.

② Click the page group's Expand button to display the subpages.

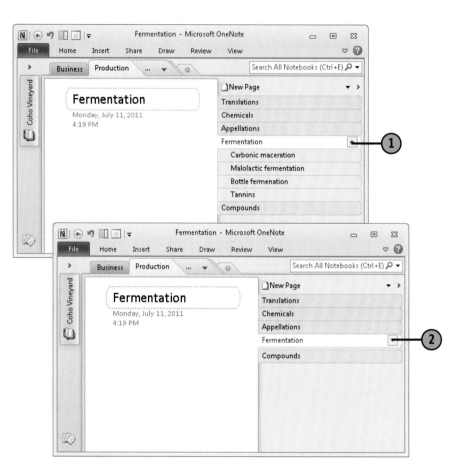

Revisiting and Restoring a Different Version of a Page

OneNote keeps back-copies of pages in case you want to revisit or restore an earlier version of a page. After you open a version of a page, you can restore it, making it the primary copy, or copy it to another section.

What's more, you can delete a version of a page, all the pages in a section, or all the pages in a notebook, and tell OneNote not to keep page versions in a notebook.

To view a version of a page, display the page, click the Share tab, and click the Page Versions button. Tabs with dated versions of your page appear in the page tabs. By clicking a page version tab, you can open a different version of a page.

After you open a page version, you can click at the top of the page to display a menu with commands for restoring, deleting, and copying the page version.

On the Share tab, the gallery on the Page Versions button offers commands for deleting versions of a page in a section, section group, or notebook, and for disabling the back-copying of pages.

Revisit and Restore a Page Version

1. Open the page you want to revisit.
2. Click the Share tab.
3. Click the Page Versions button.
4. Select a version page tab.
5. Examine the earlier version of the page.
6. Click above the page to see the page version menu.
7. Choose Restore Version.
8. Click the Page Versions button (this button is a toggle, and clicking it again hides the page versions).

See Also

"Moving, Copying, and Merging Pages and Sections" on page 132 to learn how to copy a version of a page to a different section (start by choosing Copy Page To).

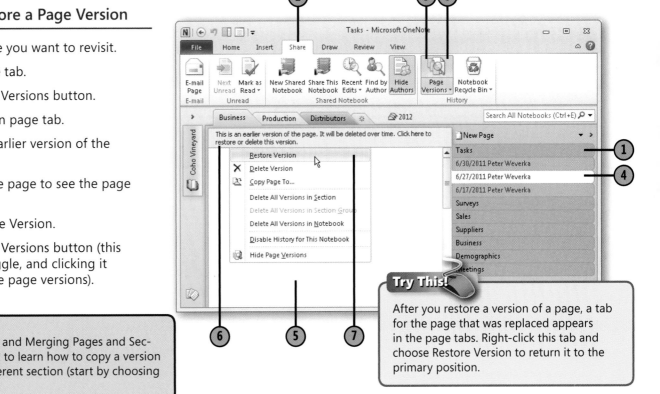

Try This!

After you restore a version of a page, a tab for the page that was replaced appears in the page tabs. Right-click this tab and choose Restore Version to return it to the primary position.

Delete Page Versions

① Click the Share tab.

② Open the gallery on the Page Versions button.

③ Choose Delete All Versions in Section.

Tip ✓

To stop keeping versions of pages throughout a notebook, open the gallery on the Page Versions button and choose Disable History for This Notebook. Beware, however, that OneNote does not keep backup copies of the notebook, not just its pages, if you choose this command.

Tip ✓

To delete individual versions of a page, click the Page Versions button. Then, in the page tabs, right-click the version you want to delete and choose Delete Version.

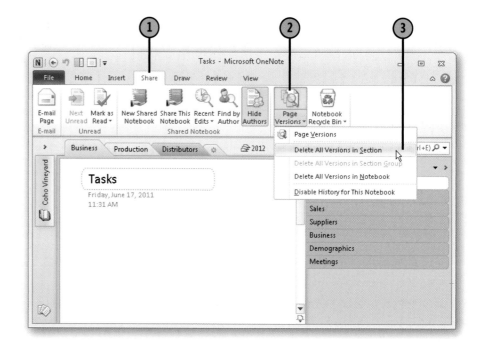

Password-Protecting a Section

Password-protect a section if you want to control who can read its pages. Before you password-protect a section, consider these password restrictions:

- In order to search password-protected sections, you must open them first and conduct your search within ten minutes (you can change this setting on the Advanced tab of the OneNote Options dialog box).

- You can't assign a password to a section with audio or video recordings.

- You can't share password-protected sections with OneNote Web App.

- Passwords are case-sensitive (you must enter, and remember, the right combination of upper- and lowercase letters).

To password-protect a section, right-click its section tab and choose Password Protect This Section. Then, in the Password Protection task pane,

Password-Protect a Section

1. Right-click the section tab of the section you want to password-protect.

2. Choose Password Protect This Section on the shortcut menu.

3. In the Password Protection task pane, click the Set Password button.

4. In the Password Protection dialog box, enter a password, enter it again for confirmation purposes, and click OK.

5. If the Existing Section Backups dialog box appears, click Delete Existing Backups.

click the Set Password button, enter the password twice in the Password Protection dialog box, and click OK.

Remove a password in the Password Protection task pane by clicking the Remove Password button.

To determine how long sections are unlocked and available for searching after you enter the password, click the File tab and choose Options. Then, in the Advanced category of the OneNote Options dialog box, choose a setting in the Lock Password Protected Sections After I Have Worked on Them menu.

Open a Password-Protected Section

1. Click the section tab.

2. Click on the screen or press Enter.

3. Enter the password in the Protect Section dialog box.

4. Click OK.

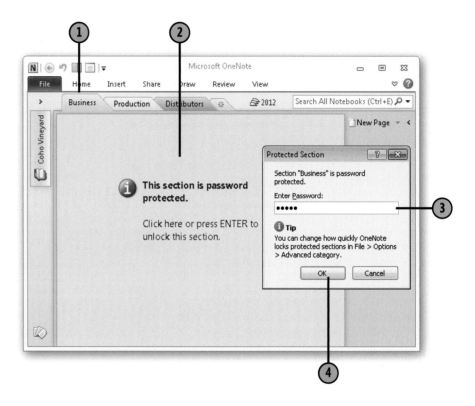

Remove a Password

1. Right-click the section tab.

2. Choose Password Protect This Section.

3. In the Password Protection task pane, click the Remove Password button.

4. In the Remove Password dialog box, enter the password and click OK.

Tip ✓

To change a password, click the Change Password button in the Password Protection task pane, enter the old password, enter the new password twice, and click OK.

5

Writing Basic Notes

The simplest type of note is a typewritten note—one you enter with the keyboard. Entering this kind of note is simple because all you have to do is click in a page and start typing.

Pages tend to get crowded with notes. To prevent over-crowding, you can move notes and delete the ones you no longer need.

The standard techniques for copying and moving text in Microsoft Office 2010 also apply in Microsoft OneNote 2010, in which you'll find the Cut, Copy, and Paste buttons on the Home tab. You'll also find standard commands for formatting text on the Home tab. For example, the Font menu, Bold button, and Italic button are located on the Home tab. OneNote 2010, like Microsoft Word 2010 and Microsoft PowerPoint 2010, has a Style menu for quickly formatting text.

Want to create a numbered or bulleted list? You can do that as well in OneNote 2010 with the Bullets and Numbering buttons on the Home tab.

Writing a Note with the Keyboard

All you have to do to write a note is click in a OneNote page and start typing. OneNote creates a *note container* for each note you write. As you write, the note container changes size to accommodate the text. A note can be as short or long as you want it to be.

A note is similar to a page in a Word 2010 document in that you can add paragraphs and align paragraphs in different ways. You can also control how much space appears between paragraphs.

The following two tables describe paragraph-alignment and paragraph-spacing options.

Paragraph Alignment Options

Align Left	Aligns the paragraph with the left side of the note container
Center	Centers the paragraph across the note container
Align Right	Aligns the paragraph with the right side of the note container

Paragraph Spacing Options

Before	Determines the amount of blank space above the paragraph (you enter the amount of space in points)
After	Determines the amount of blank space below the paragraph (in points)
Line Spacing at Least	Enters enough space above the paragraph to accommodate the largest-size letter

Tip

To format more than one paragraph at a time, select all or part of the paragraphs before choosing a formatting command. You can select more than one paragraph by dragging.

See Also

"Handwriting Notes and Converting Them to Text" on page 61 to learn how to write notes with a pen device.

Write a Note

1 Click in a page and type **Ice Cream** to create a note.

2 Press Enter to start a new paragraph and type **I scream, you scream** (and notice how the note container widens to accommodate the text).

3 Press Enter to start a third paragraph and type **We all scream for ice cream**.

4 Move the pointer over the right side of the note container; when the pointer changes to a double arrow, click and drag to the right to widen the note.

5 Click anywhere in the first paragraph.

6 Click the Home tab (if necessary).

7 Click Paragraph Alignment and choose Center to center the first paragraph.

8 Click Paragraph Alignment and choose Paragraph Spacing Options.

9 In the Paragraph Spacing dialog box, enter 14 in the After box.

10 Click OK to put 14 points of spacing between the first and second paragraph.

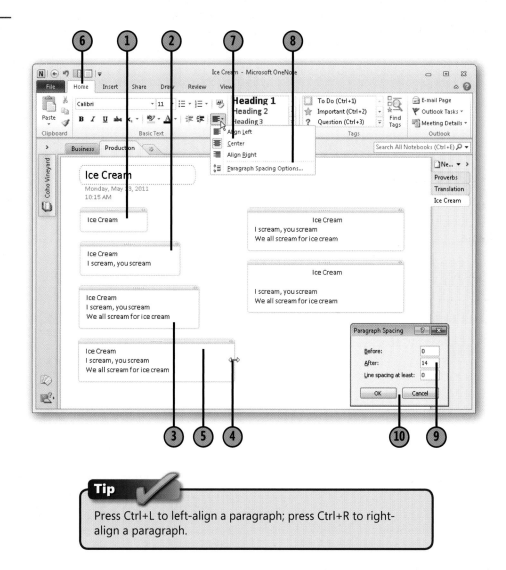

Tip

Press Ctrl+L to left-align a paragraph; press Ctrl+R to right-align a paragraph.

Selecting, Moving, and Deleting Notes

As a page starts to get crowded with notes, you have to move the notes around in order to read them. Sometimes you have to delete them as well. However, before you can move or delete a note, you have to select it.

The trick to selecting a note is to click the bar along its top. You can tell when the pointer is over this bar because it turns into the four-headed arrow pointer.

OneNote offers a quick way to move several notes lower on a page: the Insert Space button. You can also move several notes by selecting them and dragging.

Select, Move, and Delete Notes

1 Move the pointer over the bar along the top of a note; to select the note, click when you see the four-headed pointer.

2 Drag the note to move it to a different location.

3 Right-click the bar along the top of a note and choose Delete (or press the Delete key).

4 Click Undo to restore the note you deleted.

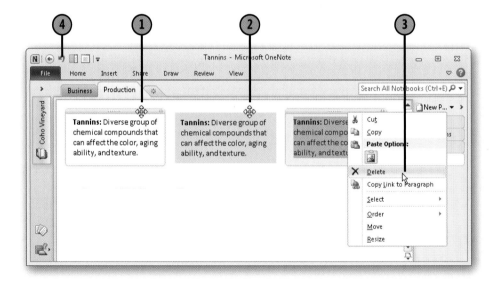

Tip

You can also use the Insert Space button to put horizontal space between notes. After clicking the Insert Space button, drag sideways.

(5) Ctrl+click the note bars on more than one note to select all the notes.

(6) Drag one of the notes you selected to move all the notes.

(7) Click the Insert tab.

(8) Click Insert Space.

(9) Drag downward on the page to insert space and move notes downward.

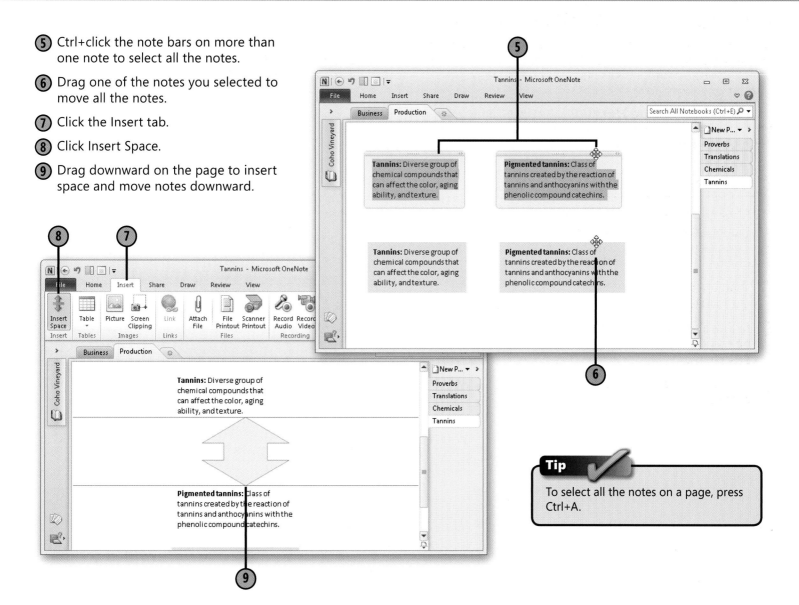

Tip

To select all the notes on a page, press Ctrl+A.

Entering Symbols and Unusual Characters

What to do when you need to enter a symbol or unusual character that isn't on the keyboard? For those times, look to the Symbol gallery and Symbol dialog box.

The Symbol gallery lists the previous 20 unusual characters and symbols you entered. If the character or symbol you need isn't there, you can probably find it in the Symbol dialog box.

Enter a Symbol or an Unusual Character

1. Click the Insert tab.

2. Click Symbol.

3. Choose a symbol or character on the gallery to insert it in a note.

4. Click Symbol and choose More Symbols.

5. Scroll through the Symbol dialog box to get a sense of all the symbols and unusual characters that are available.

6. Select a symbol or character.

7. Click Insert.

8. Click Close to close the Symbol dialog box.

9. Click Symbol and notice that the symbol or character you just chose is now on the gallery in case you want to choose it again.

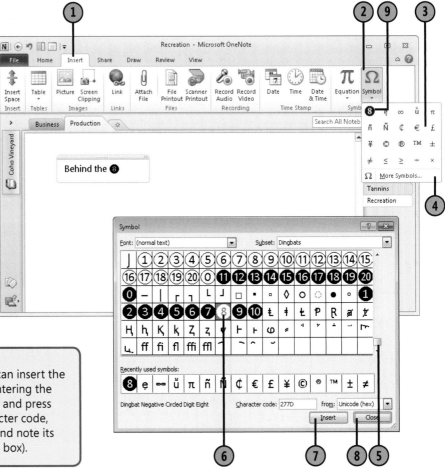

Try This!

If you know a character's Unicode character code, you can insert the character without opening the Symbol dialog box by entering the code and then pressing Alt+X. For example, enter 00BD and press Alt+X to enter the character ½. To find a Unicode character code, select a symbol or character in the Symbol dialog box and note its character code (it's listed near the bottom of the dialog box).

Selecting Text

Before you can do anything to text in a note—copy it, move it, or reformat it—you have to select it. OneNote offers a handful of techniques for selecting text (you can tell when text is selected because OneNote highlights it):

To select	Do this
A word	Double-click the word
Some text	Drag across the text
To the beginning of a line	Press Shift+Home
To the end of a line	Press Shift+End
A paragraph	Triple-click the paragraph or press Shift+Down Arrow with the cursor at the start of the paragraph
Current paragraph and subordinate paragraphs (if any)	Click the line's outline handle or press Ctrl+Shift+-

Select Text

(1) Double-click a word in a note to select it.

(2) Drag across some text to select it.

(3) Triple-click a paragraph to select it.

(4) Click a paragraph's outline handle to select it (the outline handle appears when you move the pointer to the left of the line).

See Also

"Creating and Constructing Outlines" on page 62 to learn how to use the outline handle to manipulate an item in an outline.

(1)

To be, or not to be, that is the question:
Whether 'tis nobler in the mind to suffer
The slings and arrows of outrageous fortune,
Or to take arms against a sea of troubles,
And by opposing end them?

(2)

To be, or not to be, that is the question:
Whether 'tis nobler in the mind to suffer
The slings and arrows of outrageous fortune,
Or to take arms against a sea of troubles,
And by opposing end them?

(3)

To be, or not to be, that is the question:
Whether 'tis nobler in the mind to suffer
The slings and arrows of outrageous fortune,
Or to take arms against a sea of troubles,
And by opposing end them?

(4)

To be, or not to be, that is the question:
Whether 'tis nobler in the mind to suffer
The slings and arrows of outrageous fortune,
Or to take arms against a sea of troubles,
And by opposing end them?

Copying and Moving Text

OneNote offers a number of ways to copy and move text from one place to another in a note and from one note to another. After you select the text, do the following:

- Click Copy, Cut, and Paste on the Home tab.

- Right-click and choose Cut, Copy, and Paste.

- Drag text to move it.

Copying and moving text with the Copy and Cut buttons (or their keyboard shortcuts) entails copying text to the Clipboard and then pasting it with a Paste command.

Button	Shortcut key	Description
Copy	Ctrl+C	Copy selected text to the Clipboard.
Cut	Ctrl+X	Cut selected text to the Clipboard.
Paste	Ctrl+V	Paste text from the Clipboard. OneNote offers these options for pasting: • Keep Source Formatting: The text keeps its original formatting. • Merge Formatting: The text adopts the formatting of the text where it is copied or moved. • Keep Text Only: The text is stripped of all formatting. • Picture: The text is rendered in the form of a graphic.

Tip

You can move a paragraph up or down in a note by dragging its outline handle or pressing Alt+Shift+Up Arrow or Alt+Shift+Down Arrow.

See Also

"Selecting Text" on page 49 to learn how to select text in a note.

Copy and Move Text

① Click the Home tab.

② Select text in a note.

③ Click Cut (or press Ctrl+C).

④ Move the pointer to a different location in the note, right-click, and under Paste Options on the shortcut menu, choose Keep Source Formatting to paste the text with the formatting intact.

⑤ Select text in a note.

⑥ Press Ctrl+C to copy the text to the Clipboard.

⑦ Move the pointer to a different location in the note, right-click, and under Paste Options on the shortcut menu, choose Merge Formatting to paste the text with the formatting of surrounding text.

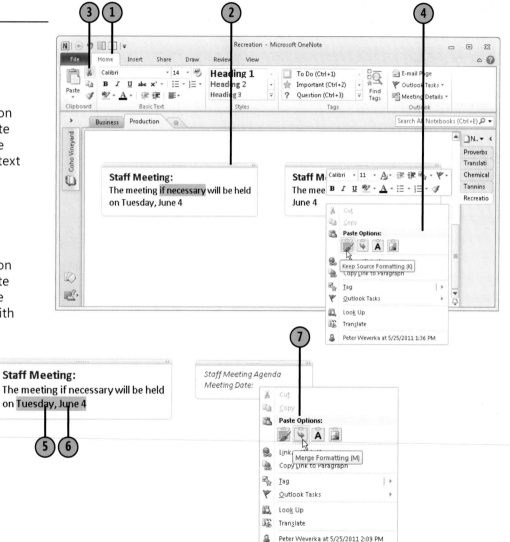

Formatting Text

Take a look at the Basic Text area of the Home tab to see the different tools for formatting text in notes. Do these tools look familiar? If you have any experience with Word, you recognize the Font menu, Font Size menu, and font style buttons: Bold, Italic, Underline, and Strikethrough. The formatting tools and their shortcut keys work the same way in OneNote and Word.

OneNote gives you these opportunities to format text:

Menu/Button	Shortcut key	Description
Font		Choose a font (a typeface)
Font Size		Shrink or enlarge the text
Bold	Ctrl+B	Boldface the text
Italic	Ctrl+I	Italicize the text
Underline	Ctrl+U	Underline the text
Strikethrough	Ctrl+-	Draw a line through the text
Subscript/Superscript	Ctrl+=; Ctrl+Shift+=	Lower or raise the text from the baseline (the imaginary line that the letters rest on)
Text Highlight Color	Ctrl+Shift+H (for yellow)	Highlight text
Font Color		Change the color of text

To use the formatting tools, do one of the following:

- Select a formatting menu option or click a formatting button and then start typing.

- Select the text first and then select a formatting menu option or click a formatting button.

OneNote offers a special button for stripping all formats from text: the Clear Formatting button (press Ctrl+Shift+N). Click this button to wipe the slate clean and start all over with formatting text.

Tip ✓

A quick way to format text is to use the Format Painter. Click in text with formatting that you want to apply elsewhere. Then, on the Home tab, click the Format Painter button and click or drag across the text to which you want to copy the formats.

Format Text

(1) Click the Home tab.

(2) Triple-click a word to select the entire paragraph in which it is located.

(3) Click Bold (or press Ctrl+B) to bold-face the text.

(4) Click Italic (or press Ctrl+I) to italicize the text.

(5) Click Clear Formatting (or press Ctrl+Shift+N) to remove the boldface and italics from the text.

(6) Open the Font menu and choose a different font.

(7) Open the Font Size menu and choose a different font size.

(8) Open the Font Color menu and choose a different font color.

(9) Click Clear Formatting (or press Ctrl+Shift+N).

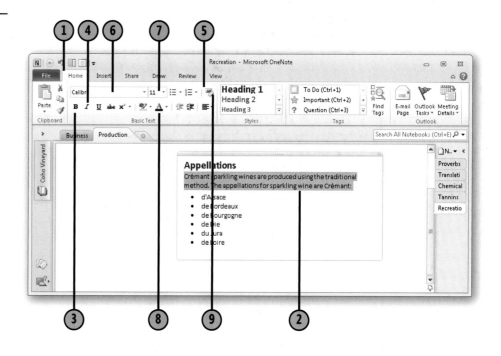

See Also

"Applying Styles to Text" on page 54 to learn how to format text quickly with a style.

Tip ✓

To change the default font, font size, and font color, click the File tab and choose Options. In the Options dialog box, go to the General category and choose default fonts.

Applying Styles to Text

The fastest way to reformat text in a note is to choose a style from the Styles menu on the Home tab. OneNote offers 11 styles in all. Six of the styles (Heading 1 through Heading 6) are for formatting headings in notes. Normal is the default style, the one that is used when you create a new note. OneNote also provides the Citation style for citations, the Quote style for quotations, and the Code style for computer code. However, you can use these styles any way you want.

Styles apply to paragraphs, not to individual words or letters. To apply a style, just click in a paragraph and choose a style from the Styles menu on the Home tab (or press a keyboard shortcut). The style applies to all text in the paragraph.

Apply Styles to Text

1. Click the Home tab.

2. Click in a paragraph in a note.

3. Open the Styles menu and choose Heading 1 (or press Ctrl+Alt+1).

4. Open the Styles menu and choose Citation.

5. Open the Styles menu and choose Quote.

6. Open the Styles menu and choose Code.

7. Open the Styles menu and choose Normal (or press Ctrl+Shift+N).

OneNote offers these keyboard shortcuts for applying styles:

Press	To apply this style
Ctrl+Alt+1 through Ctrl+Alt+6	Heading 1 through 6
Ctrl+Shift+N	Normal

Tip ✓

To apply a style to more than one paragraph, select the paragraphs before applying the style.

Creating Numbered and Bulleted Lists

Lists are invaluable for keeping information in notes. Use numbered lists to rank items in a list or describe step-by-step instructions. Use bulleted lists to present alternatives or list unranked items.

In OneNote, you don't have to enter the numbers or bullets yourself. After you click the Numbering or Bullets button on the Home tab, OneNote numbers the list or applies bullets for you. You can choose from several numbering schemes and bullet styles.

To create a numbered or bulleted list, use one of these techniques:

Create a Numbered List

① Type several items for a list, pressing Enter after you enter each item.

② Click the Home tab.

③ Select the list items.

④ Click the Numbering button (or press Ctrl+/) to create a numbered list from the items.

⑤ Open the gallery on the Numbering button and choose an alternative numbering scheme.

⑥ Right-click a number in the middle of the list and choose Remove Number on the shortcut menu.

⑦ Right-click the following number in the list and choose Begin a New List Here on the shortcut menu.

(continued on next page)

- Enter items for the list, select the list, and then click the Numbering or Bullets button on the Home tab.

- Click the Numbering or Bullets button on the Home tab and then enter list items. Each time you press the Enter key to start a new line, OneNote applies a number or bullet to the list item.

On the shortcut menu, OneNote offers commands for starting new lists, continuing previous lists, removing numbers or bullets from lists, and changing numbered lists to bulleted lists and vice versa.

Create a Numbered List *(continued)*

⑧ Select the list.

⑨ Open the gallery on the Numbering button and choose None (or press Ctrl+/) to remove all numbers from the list.

Create a Bulleted List

① Type several items for a list, pressing Enter after you enter each item.

② Click the Home tab.

③ Select the items in the list.

④ Click the Bullets button (or press Ctrl+.) to create a bulleted list.

⑤ Open the drop-down menu on the Bullets button and choose a different bullet style.

⑥ With the bulleted list still selected, click the Bullets button (or press Ctrl+.) to remove the bullets from the list.

Try This!

Type an asterisk (*) and press the Spacebar. OneNote automatically creates a bulleted list. After you enter list items and press Enter, OneNote attaches a bullet to each item on the list. You can use this simple method to create bulleted lists.

Try This!

Type 1 and press the Spacebar. OneNote automatically creates a numbered list for you. After you enter the first list item and press Enter, OneNote enters a 2 for the second item in the list. You can use this automatic technique to create numbered lists.

See Also

"Creating and Constructing Outlines" on page 62 to learn how to create another kind of numbered list: an outline.

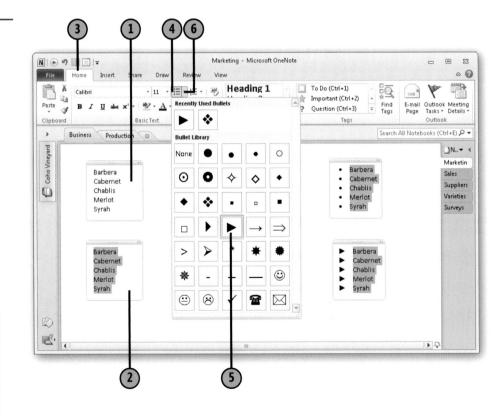

6

Taking Notes to Another Level

Typewritten notes aren't the only kind of notes you can write. Far from it. You can also handwrite notes and convert them to text, record audio notes, and record video notes.

Microsoft OneNote 2010 also comes with special tools for constructing outlines and math equations.

To get information from elsewhere for a note, consider attaching a file to a note, showing the printout of a file in a note, and scanning documents and putting the scanned images in notes.

OneNote 2010 makes it easy to put pictures and screen shots in notes, too.

When you're in a hurry to write a note or you haven't decided yet where to store one, write a side note. You can store side notes temporarily in the Unfiled Notes folder until you find a permanent place for them.

Writing Side Notes

When you want to jot down a note but can't decide where to store it, or you want to jot down a note without first opening OneNote 2010, write a *side note*. Side notes are kept one to a page in the Unfiled Notes folder until you delete them or move them elsewhere.

Use these techniques to open the Side Note window and write a side note:

- When OneNote is open, go to the View tab and click the New Side Note button (or press Ctrl+Shift+M).

- When OneNote is closed or open, click the Open New Side Note icon in the notification area of the Windows taskbar (or press Windows key+N). The notification area is located in the lower-right corner of the screen, next to the clock (you may have to click the Show Hidden Icons button in the notification area to see all the icons).

The Side Note window offers the Home, Draw, and View tabs for formatting, drawing, and viewing side notes as you write them. Use the Pages tab to read, search for, create, delete, and move side notes. Click the Close button to close the Side Note window after you write your side note.

To read side notes, open OneNote (if necessary) and click Unfiled Notes at the bottom of the Navigation bar. The Unfiled Notes folder opens. Side notes are stored one to a page in this folder. Use these techniques to manage pages in the Unfiled Notes folder:

- Reading: Click a page tab to read a note.

- Moving and copying: Right-click a page tab, and choose Move or Copy to move or copy a page from the Unfiled Notes folder to a notebook.

- Deleting: Right-click a page tab and choose Delete to delete a note.

Write a Side Note

1. Click the View tab.
2. Click the New Side Note button.
3. Write the side note.
4. Click Close to close the window.
5. In the Notification area, click the Open New Side Note icon.
6. Write another side note.
7. Click the Expand the Ribbon button.
8. Click the Pages tab.
9. Click Previous Page to see your previous side note.
10. Click Close.

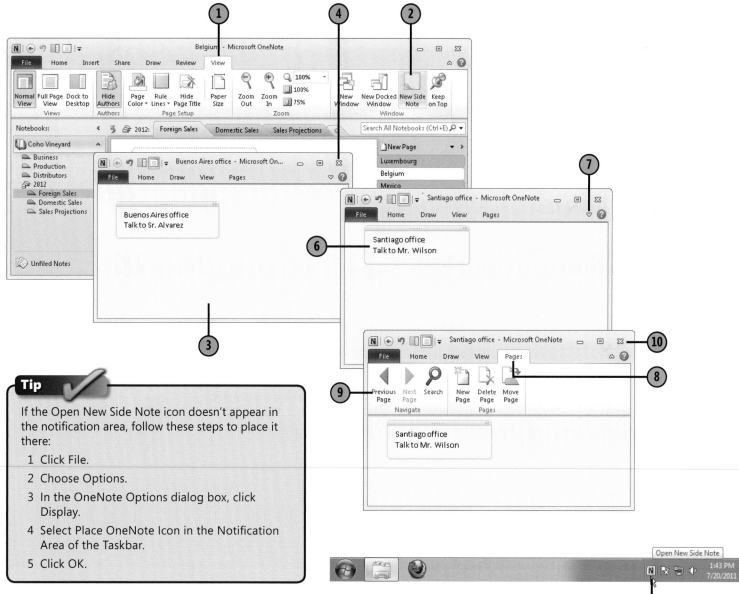

Tip

If the Open New Side Note icon doesn't appear in the notification area, follow these steps to place it there:

1 Click File.

2 Choose Options.

3 In the OneNote Options dialog box, click Display.

4 Select Place OneNote Icon in the Notification Area of the Taskbar.

5 Click OK.

Manage Side Notes in the Unfiled Notes Folder

(1) In the Navigation bar, click Unfiled Notes.

(2) Click a page tab to read a note.

(3) Drag a page tab to a section in the Navigation bar to move a page to a section in an open notebook.

(4) Right-click a page tab and choose Delete to delete a side note.

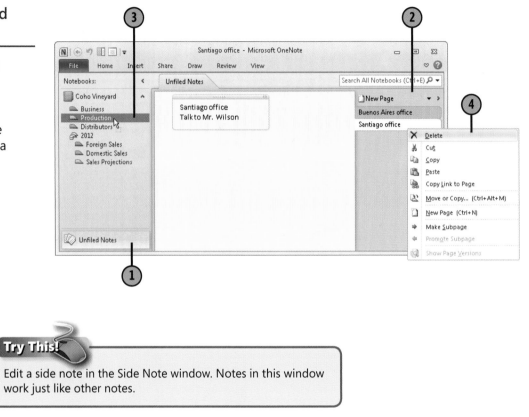

Try This!

Edit a side note in the Side Note window. Notes in this window work just like other notes.

Handwriting Notes and Converting Them to Text

People with tablet PCs, touch-enabled PCs, or pen devices can handwrite notes. To do so, go to the Draw tab, select a pen and pen color, and drag your pen device on the pad or finger on the screen. (You can also, with unsatisfactory results, handwrite notes by dragging the mouse.)

When OneNote recognizes what it thinks are handwritten notes on a page, the Ink to Text button on the Draw tab becomes available for clicking. When this button is available, use one of these techniques to convert all handwritten notes on the page to text:

Handwrite a Note and Convert It to Text

1 Click the Draw tab.

2 Select a pen (not a highlighter) from the Pens gallery.

3 Using a pen device, your finger, or the mouse, drag to handwrite a note.

4 Click the Ink to Text button to convert the note to text.

See Also

"Drawing Free-Form with a Pen or Highlighter" on page 116 to learn how to choose a pen size and pen color for drawing and handwriting notes.

Caution

If you can't handwrite notes, OneNote isn't in Create Handwriting Only mode or Create Both Handwriting and Drawings mode. To change pen modes, open the Pens gallery, choose Pen Mode, and choose an option.

- Click the Ink to Text button on the Draw tab.

- Right-click a handwritten note, choose Convert Ink on the shortcut menu, and choose Ink to Text on the submenu.

Click the Select & Type button on the Draw tab when you finish handwriting notes and want to resume typing them.

To be able to handwrite notes, OneNote must be in Create Handwriting Only mode or Create Both Handwriting and Drawings mode. To choose a pen mode, open the Pens gallery on the Draw tab, select Pen Mode, and choose an option on the submenu.

Creating and Constructing Outlines

An outline is a list of important topics in a given subject. In a typical outline, topics are listed at different levels, with first-level topics not indented and sublevel topics indented to show they are subordinate.

To create an outline, enter the topics in a list with one topic per line. Then, to show which topics are subtopics, indent the subtopics. To number the outline, either select the list and click the Numbering button or click the Numbering button before you start entering topics and subtopics (the Numbering button is located on the Home tab).

To help construct outlines, OneNote offers the paragraph selection handle. Move the pointer over a paragraph to make its paragraph selection handle appear on the left. Do the following with the paragraph selection handle to construct an outline:

- Change the indentation level: Drag the handle to the left or right to indent a topic. You can also press Tab or click the Increase Indent Position button on the Home tab to move a topic to a lower level; press Shift+Tab

or click the Decrease Indent Position button to raise a subtopic to a higher level.

- Move a topic higher or lower in the outline: Drag the paragraph selection handle up or down in the note.

- Select a topic and its subtopics: Click the paragraph selection handle.

- Collapse or expand a topic's subtopics: Double-click the paragraph selection handle. You can also press Alt+Shift+minus sign to collapse or Alt+Shift+plus sign to expand subtopics.

- Select topics at different levels: Right-click the paragraph selection handle, choose Select, and choose a level on the submenu. Select all topics on the same level when you want to format text. For example, to italicize all level-3 subtopics, select them and click the Italic button.

Paragraph selection handle

Click to select subtopics

Double-click to collapse/expand subtopics

Right-click to select topic levels

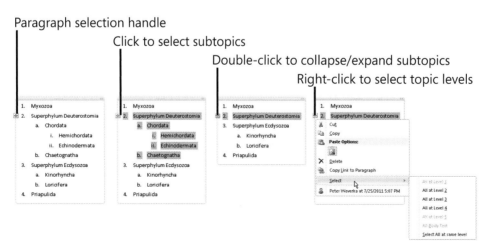

Create and Construct an Outline

(1) Create the initial outline by entering a six-item list.

(2) Select the list and press Ctrl+/ (or click the Numbering button on the Home tab).

(3) Drag over parts of the second and third item so that all or part of each item is selected.

(4) Drag the paragraph selection handle to the right to indent items 2 and 3 in the outline.

(5) Drag the paragraph selection handle on item 1 downward until item 1 becomes item 4 in the outline.

(6) Double-click the paragraph selection handle on item 4 to collapse its subtopics.

(7) Right-click any paragraph selection handle in the outline, choose Select, and choose All at Level 2.

(8) Press Ctrl+B to bold all level-2 topics in the outline.

(9) Double-click the paragraph selection handle on item 4 to expand its subtopics.

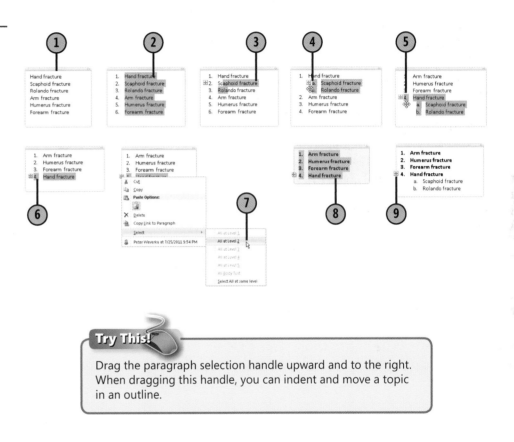

Try This!

Drag the paragraph selection handle upward and to the right. When dragging this handle, you can indent and move a topic in an outline.

Date- and Time-Stamping Notes

Date- and time-stamp notes to record when they were written. Or use the date- and time-stamping commands to insert the date, time, or date and time in the middle of a note you're writing.

To date- and time-stamp notes, go to the Insert tab and click a button: Date (or press Alt+Shift+D), Time (or press Alt+Shift+T), or Date & Time (or press Alt+Shift+F).

Date- and Time-Stamp a Note

① Click the Insert tab.

② Click Date.

③ Click Time.

④ Click Date & Time.

Tip

To insert your name, the current date, and the current time, right-click and choose the last option on the shortcut menu.

Placing Files and Printouts in Notes

OneNote offers three commands for importing files into a notebook. These commands are available on the Insert tab:

- Attach File: Embeds files with a notebook. After you attach a file, double-click its shortcut icon to open it.

- File Printout: Inserts files so that you can read and search (but not edit) their content in OneNote.

- Scanner Printout: Imports scanned paper documents and digital photos into OneNote so that you can view their content.

Attach a File to a Note

① Click the Insert tab.

② Click Attach File.

③ Select the file in the Choose a File dialog box (Ctrl+click to select more than one file).

④ Click Insert.

Try This!

Move the pointer over the attached file icon. A ScreenTip shows you the file's name, when it was last modified, the folder from which it was originally copied, and its size.

See Also

"Creating Links to Web Pages and Files" on page 87 to learn how to link a note to a file so that you can open and edit a file by clicking its link in OneNote.

Attaching a File to a Note

Attach a file to a note to preserve a copy of a file or make the file available in your notebook. After you attach a file, you can double-click its icon to open it.

Attached files are embedded in notebooks; they are not linked to their original versions. Editorial changes you make to the original file don't appear in the attachment file; changes you make to the attachment file don't transfer to the original.

To attach a file to a note, go to the Insert tab and click the Attach File button. Then, in the Choose a File dialog box, select the file and click the Insert button. You can insert more than one file in a note with the Attach File command.

Inserting a File Printout

Insert a file printout to copy a text file into OneNote and retain all the text formatting. After you insert the text file, you can read and search it, but not edit it.

Besides inserting the file text, OneNote inserts a shortcut icon to the file and a link to the file. You can double-click the shortcut icon or click the file link to open the file in its default application.

To insert a file printout, go to the Insert tab and click the File Printout button. Then select a text file in the Choose a File dialog box and click the Insert button.

Insert a File Printout

1. Click the Insert tab.

2. Click File Printout.

3. Select the file in the Choose Document to Insert dialog box.

4. Click Insert.

5. Double-click the file's shortcut icon to open the file in its default application.

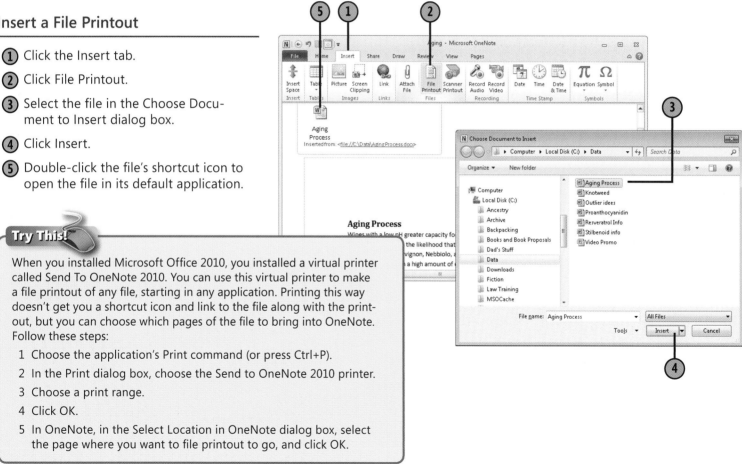

Try This!

When you installed Microsoft Office 2010, you installed a virtual printer called Send To OneNote 2010. You can use this virtual printer to make a file printout of any file, starting in any application. Printing this way doesn't get you a shortcut icon and link to the file along with the printout, but you can choose which pages of the file to bring into OneNote. Follow these steps:

1 Choose the application's Print command (or press Ctrl+P).

2 In the Print dialog box, choose the Send to OneNote 2010 printer.

3 Choose a print range.

4 Click OK.

5 In OneNote, in the Select Location in OneNote dialog box, select the page where you want to file printout to go, and click OK.

Inserting Content from a Scanner or Digital Camera

Use the Scanner Printout command to scan paper documents from a scanner or photos from a digital camera and place an image of the document or photos in OneNote.

To start, make sure that the scanner or digital camera is plugged into one of your computer's USB ports. Then go to the Insert tab and click Scanner Printout. The Insert Picture from Scanner or Camera dialog box appears. Choose a device and resolution setting, and click Insert to begin scanning or Custom Insert to select more scanning options.

Insert Content from a Scanner or Digital Camera

① Click the Insert tab.

② Click Scanner Printout.

③ In the Insert Picture from Scanner or Camera dialog box, select a device and resolution.

④ Click Custom Insert.

⑤ In the Scan Using dialog box, click Preview.

⑥ Click Scan.

Tip

You can change the size of a scanned image. Move the pointer over the lower-right corner; when you see the two-headed arrow, click and start dragging.

Tip

Select Add Pictures to Clip Organizer in the Insert Picture from Scanner or Camera dialog box to place the image in the Microsoft Clip Organizer. The Clip Organizer is an application for storing and editing images. To open it, click the Start button, choose All Programs, choose Microsoft Office, choose Microsoft Office 2010 Tools, and choose Microsoft Clip Organizer.

Placing Images in Notes

On the Insert tab, OneNote offers two commands for placing images in notes:

- Picture: Insert a JPEG, PNG, TIFF, or other digital image.
- Screen Clipping: Take a screen clipping, a screen shot of part of any open window on your computer screen.

Pictures and screen clippings are images. You can change the size of a picture or screen clipping by dragging its lower-right corner.

Insert a Picture

1. Click the Insert tab.
2. Click Picture.
3. In the Insert Picture dialog box, select a picture.
4. Click Insert.

Tip

Ctrl+click pictures in the Insert Picture dialog box to select and insert more than one picture.

Inserting a Picture

To insert a picture, go to the Insert tab and click Picture. The Insert Picture dialog box appears. Select a picture and click Insert.

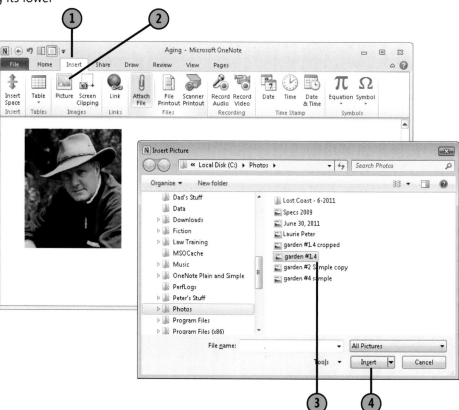

Taking a Screen Clipping

To capture part of an open window on your computer as a screen shot, take a *screen clipping*. For example, capture part of a web page or application screen in a screen clipping.

Before you begin, display the item that you want to capture on your screen. For example, to capture part of a web page, display the web page in your browser. Then switch to OneNote, go to the Insert tab, and click Screen Clipping (or press Windows key+S). You return to the application you were in previously. Drag the pointer across the part of the screen you want for your clipping. You return to OneNote, where the screen clipping appears in a note along with a notice saying when it was taken (a URL appears as well if the clipping was taken from a web page).

Take a Screen Clipping

① Display the web page, file, or application window you want to capture.

② In OneNote, click the Insert tab.

③ Click Screen Clipping.

④ Drag on the screen to define which portion of the screen you want to capture.

The other way to create a screen clipping is to right-click the OneNote icon in the notification area of the taskbar and choose Create Screen Clipping. After you drag to capture part of the screen, the Select Location in OneNote dialog box appears so you can choose a page for the screen clipping.

Tip

If you want to take a screen clipping of the One-Note screen, display the screen and press Windows key+S or right-click the OneNote icon in the notification area and choose Create Screen Clipping. You can't do it by clicking the Screen Clipping button on the Insert tab.

Constructing Math Equations

Writing and drawing math 5equations can be difficult, and to make constructing equations a little easier, OneNote offers two techniques for putting equations in notes.

One technique is to construct an equation using the Equation Tools Design tab. On the Insert tab, click the Equation button. Then, on the Equation Tools Design tab, use the tools, symbols, and structures to fashion an equation:

- Tools: Offers commands for inserting and constructing equations, as well as converting between one- to two-dimensional displays.

- Symbols: Provides a gallery of symbols to insert in equations.

- Structures: Provides a gallery of components, including fractions, integrals, and radicals, to insert in equations.

The other technique is to draw the equation in the Insert Ink Equation dialog box. Use this technique to write simple equations. On the Draw tab, click the Ink to Math button to open the Insert Ink Equation dialog box. After you click the Insert button in this dialog box, OneNote converts your hand-drawn equation to text.

Use Equation Tools to Construct an Equation

1. Click the Insert tab.

2. Click Equation.

3. Click Fraction and choose the first fraction in the gallery.

4. In the fraction placeholders, enter **4** and **3**.

5. Click to the right of the fraction and then click the Multiplication Sign.

6. Type **6** on your keyboard.

7. Click to the right of the number 6 and click the Equal Sign.

8. Type **8** on your keyboard.

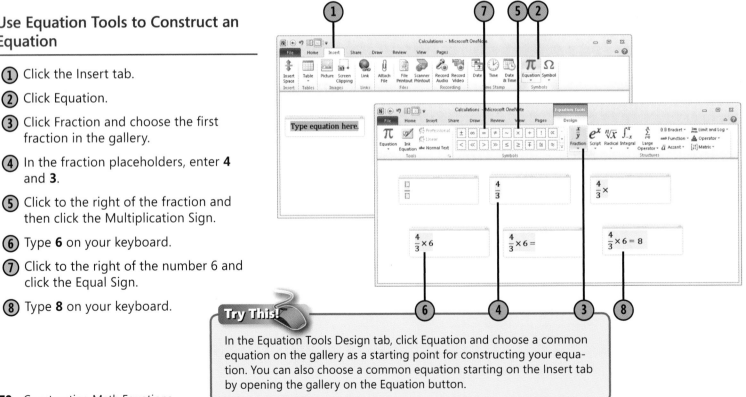

Try This!

In the Equation Tools Design tab, click Equation and choose a common equation on the gallery as a starting point for constructing your equation. You can also choose a common equation starting on the Insert tab by opening the gallery on the Equation button.

Construct an Equation in the Insert Ink Equation Window

① Click the Draw tab.

② Click the Ink to Math button.

③ Using the mouse, a pen device, or your finger, draw the following equation: **4 + 1 = 5**.

④ Look at the Preview area to see whether OneNote interpreted your drawing correctly.

⑤ Click Insert.

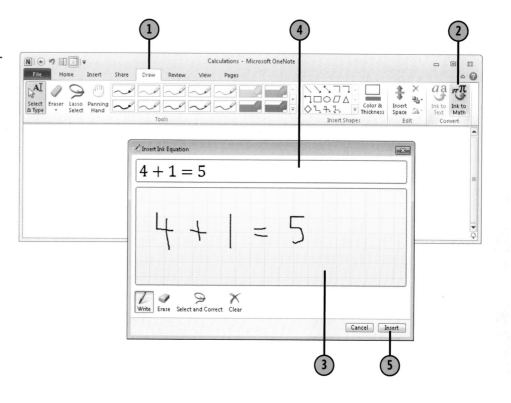

Recording Audio and Video Notes

If your computer is equipped with audio and video capability, you can record audio and video notes and play back the recordings on the Audio & Video Playback tab.

What's more, OneNote links recordings to notes you take while a recording is being made or played back, and you can click these playback links to revisit different parts of a recording. To play back your supervisor's speech at a staff meeting, for example, you can select the note that you wrote while your supervisor spoke and then click the playback link attached to the note. In this way, you can write notes about meetings and events, and use your notes as a means to return to the parts of meetings and events that you recorded.

To record an audio or video note, go to the Insert tab and click the Record Audio or Record Video button. The recording starts and the Audio & Video Recording tab opens. You can click the Pause button to pause the recording. Any notes you type during the recording are linked to the recording.

To play back an audio or video recording, open the Audio & Video Playback tab, select a recording, and click the Play button. If you wrote notes about the recording, click a note or a paragraph in a note and then click its playback link to hear or view the portion of the recording that was made while you wrote the note.

The Audio & Video Playback tab offers commands for playing, pausing, stopping, rewinding, and fast-forwarding.

To write notes about a recording you already made, play the recording and start taking notes. The notes you take will be linked to the recording.

Record an Audio or Video Note

1. Click the Insert tab.

2. Click Record Audio or Record Video.

3. Click Pause to pause the recording.

4. Click a different part of the screen to begin writing descriptions of the recording there.

5. Click Pause again to resume recording.

6. Write several descriptive paragraphs about the recording as it occurs.

7. Click Stop.

Try This!

The Audio & Video Playback tab also offers a Record Audio and Record Video button. Click one of these buttons to record another audio or video note on the page.

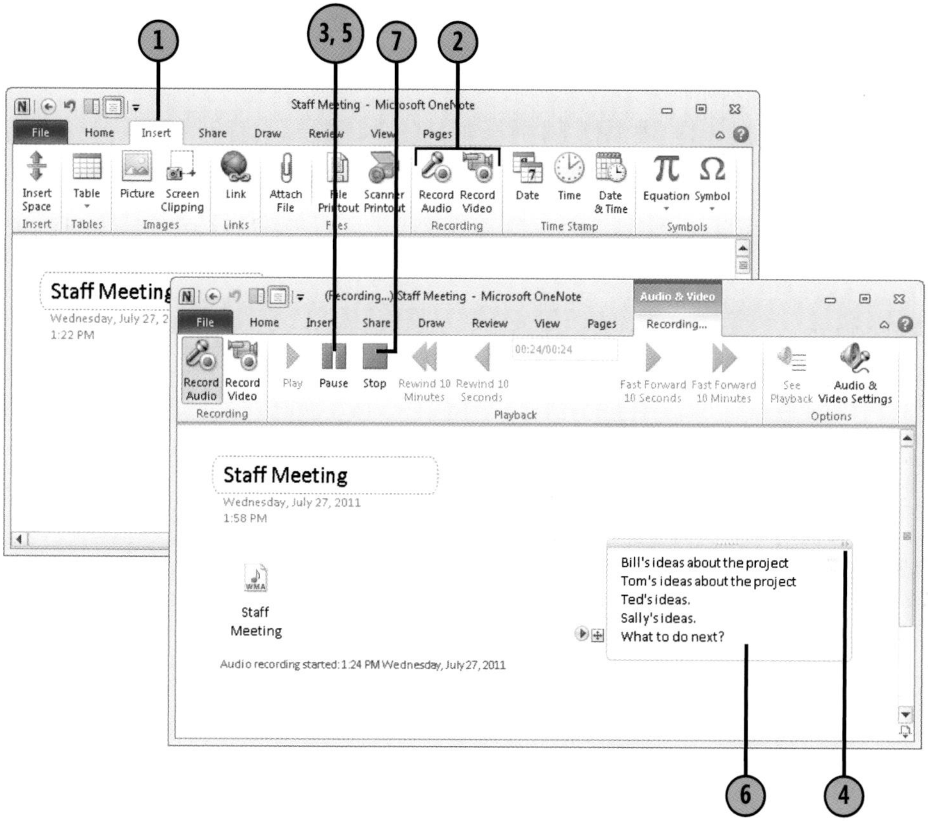
1
3, 5
7
2
Staff Meeting - Microsoft OneNote
File
Home
Insert
Share
Draw
Review
View
Pages
Insert Space
Table
Picture
Screen Clipping
Link
Attach File
File Printout
Scanner Printout
Record Audio
Record Video
Date
Time
Date & Time
Equation
Symbol
Insert
Tables
Images
Links
Files
Recording
Time Stamp
Symbols
(Recording...) Staff Meeting - Microsoft OneNote
Audio & Video
Recording...
Play
Pause
Stop
Rewind 10 Minutes
Rewind 10 Seconds
00:24/00:24
Fast Forward 10 Seconds
Fast Forward 10 Minutes
See Playback
Audio & Video Settings
Playback
Options
Staff Meeting
Wednesday, July 27, 2011
1:58 PM
Staff Meeting
Audio recording started: 1:24 PM Wednesday, July 27, 2011
Bill's ideas about the project
Tom's ideas about the project
Ted's ideas.
Sally's ideas.
What to do next?
6
4

Play Back an Audio or Video Note

1. Click the Audio & Video Playback tab.
2. Select the audio or video note.
3. Click Play on the ribbon.
4. Click Pause.
5. Click the Play button next to a paragraph or note to play one portion of the recording.

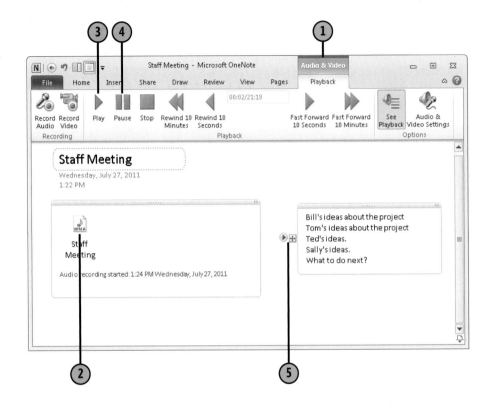

7

Putting a Table in a Note

For presenting data, it's hard to beat a table. A table gives you a concise picture of data. You can compare and contrast the numbers and tell what's what. You can see trends and tell at a glance who or what is performing well or lagging behind.

However, creating a table can be a chore. You need the correct number of columns and rows. Columns must be the right width to hold the data. You need to align the numbers and text to make the data speak.

OneNote offers all kinds of tools on the Table Tools Layout tab to help you make your tables just-so. In this section, you explore these tools. You find out how to create a table in a note, insert and delete columns and rows, and select parts of a table so you can format the table's various parts. You also see how to manage table borders, change column widths, and align the text.

Creating a Table

You can make a table a part of a note or make it a note unto itself. After you create the initial table, you can go to the Table Tools Layout tab to construct it to your liking.

Create a Table

① Click in a note (to insert a table in a note) or click the screen (to create a stand-alone table in a new note).

② Click the Insert tab.

③ Click the Table button.

④ Use one of these techniques to tell OneNote how many columns and rows you want:

- Click in the table grid.

- Click Insert Table, and in the Insert Table dialog box, enter the number of columns and rows, and click OK.

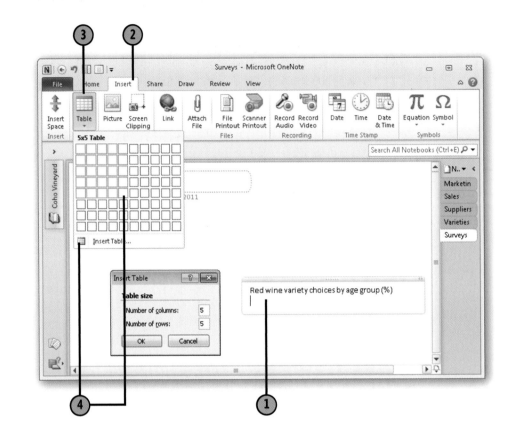

Try This!

A quick way to create a table is to type the first table entry and then press Tab. OneNote creates a simple one-row, two-column table. To add columns to this table, press Tab with the cursor in the rightmost column. After you add the columns, you can add rows by placing the cursor in the rightmost column of the last row and then pressing Enter.

Tip

To make room in a note for a table title, click to the left of the first entry in the table and press Enter. For example, if the first entry (the entry in column 1, row 1) is the word Age, click to the left of the letter A in this word and press Enter. OneNote adds space at the top of the note for a title or other text.

Inserting and Deleting Columns and Rows

Unless you are lucky or clever enough to choose the right number of columns and rows for your table when you create it, you need to add and delete columns and rows as you con-struct your table. On the Table Tools Layout tab, OneNote offers commands for adding and deleting columns and rows.

Insert a Column or Row

(1) Click in the column or row next to the column or row you want to insert.

- To insert a column, click anywhere in an existing column to the left or right of the column you want to insert.

- To insert a row, click anywhere in an existing row above or below the row you want to insert.

(2) Click the Layout tab.

(3) Click an Insert button:

- Click Insert Left (or press Ctrl+Alt+E) or Insert Right (or press Ctrl+Alt+R) to insert a column.

- Click Insert Above or Insert Below (or press Ctrl+Enter) to insert a row.

Tip ✔

You can insert more than one column or row at a time by selecting cells in more than one column or row before clicking an Insert button. For example, to insert two columns, drag the mouse to select any adjacent cells in two existing columns, and then click the Insert Left or Insert Right button.

Delete a Column or Row

① Click in the column or row you want to delete.

② Click the Layout tab.

③ Click the Delete Columns or Delete Rows button.

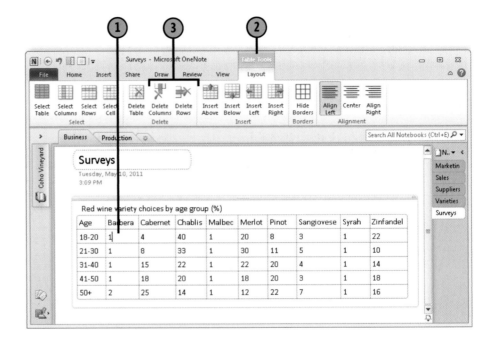

Tip

To delete more than one column or row at a time, select the columns or rows (by clicking a Select button) and then click a Delete button. You can also press Delete to delete columns or rows after you select them.

Try This!

Need to delete a table, maybe to start all over? Click anywhere in the table, click the Layout tab, and click the Delete Table button. (Click the Undo button if you regret deleting your table.)

Selecting Parts of a Table

Before you can format part of a table, you have to select it. For example, to bold text in the first row, select the first row and click the Bold button on the Home tab (or press Ctrl+B).

After you select a part of a table, it is highlighted. Formatting commands that you apply while part of a table is highlighted apply to all highlighted parts.

Select a Cell, Column, Row, or Table

① Click the part of the table you want to select. For example, to select a column or row, click anywhere in the column or row.

② Click the Layout tab.

③ Click a Select button (Select Table, Select Columns, Select Rows, or Select Cell).

Red wine variety choices by age group (%)

Age	Barbera	Cabernet	Chablis	Malbec	Merlot	Pinot	Sangiovese	Syrah	Zinfandel
21-30	1	8	33	1	30	11	5	1	10
31-40	1	15	22	1	22	20	4	1	14
41-50	1	18	20	1	18	20	3	1	18
50+	2	25	14	1	12	22	7	1	16

Tip

You can select more than one column or row by dragging across cells in more than one column or row before clicking a Select button.

Caution

You can drag over adjacent cells in a row to select them. However, dragging over adjacent cells in a column selects the adjacent cells as well as the cells throughout the rows.

Handling Table Borders

Table borders are the lines in a table that mark where rows and columns are. Borders are convenient for entering data in a table. You can see clearly where to enter each data item. But sometimes a table looks better without the borders.

By clicking the Hide Borders button on the Table Tools Layout tab, you can hide or display table borders.

Hide or Display Table Borders

1 Click anywhere in the table.

2 Click the Layout tab.

3 Click the Hide Borders button.

Age	Barbera	Cabernet	Chablis	Malbec	Merlot	Pinot	Sangiovese	Syrah	Zinfandel
21-30	1	8	33	1	30	11	5	1	10
31-40	1	15	22	1	22	20	4	1	14
41-50	1	18	20	1	18	20	3	1	18
50+	2	25	14	1	12	22	7	1	16

Red wine variety choices by age group (%)

Surveys
Tuesday, May 10, 2011
3:09 PM

Changing the Width of Columns

To make data fit more snugly in a table, sometimes it's necessary to change the width of columns and make them narrower or wider. You can do that by dragging column borders.

The only way to change the height of rows is to enlarge the text in a table. OneNote makes each row tall enough to accommodate its tallest entry. By enlarging the text, you also enlarge the row height.

Change the Width of a Column

(1) Hover the pointer over the right-side border of the column whose width you want to change.

(2) When you see the two-headed arrow cursor, click and drag to the left (to narrow the column) or to the right (to widen it).

Tip

You can widen all columns in a table by enlarging the table's note container. Drag the right side of a note container to enlarge it.

See Also

"Handling Table Borders" on page 80 to learn how to display borders in a table.

Aligning Text in Tables

Align text in a table in different ways to make the table easier to read and understand. Typically, numbers are right-aligned so that they line up under one another and can be compared more easily. Labels are typically center-aligned or left-aligned. OneNote provides Alignment buttons on the Table Tools Layout tab for aligning text.

Left-Align, Center, or Right-Align Text

1. Click anywhere in the table.

2. Click the Layout tab.

3. Select the rows, columns, or cells with the data you want to realign; or select the entire table.

4. Click an Alignment button (Align Left, Center, or Align Right).

Red wine variety choices by age group (%)

Age	Barbera	Cabernet	Chablis	Malbec	Merlot	Pinot	Sangiovese	Syrah	Zinfandel
21-30	1	8	33	1	30	11	5	1	10
31-40	1	15	22	1	22	20	4	1	14
41-50	1	18	20	1	18	20	3	1	18
50+	2	25	14	1	12	22	7	1	16

Tip

Press Ctrl+R to right-align text in cells; press Ctrl+L to left-align text.

See Also

"Selecting Parts of a Table" on page 79 to learn how to select cells, columns, rows, or an entire table.

8

Linking Your Notes

In this section:

- Linking to Other Places in OneNote
- Creating Links to Web Pages and Files
- Editing and Managing Links
- Taking Linked Notes

Microsoft OneNote 2010 offers all kinds of opportunities for linking: to other sections and pages in OneNote 2010, to web pages, and to files. With the Linked Notes feature, you can even tell OneNote to link automatically to Microsoft Word 2010 documents, Microsoft PowerPoint 2010 presentations, web pages, and other OneNote pages as you take notes.

A link is a shortcut from one place to another. Create links as a way to navigate to web pages, files, and places in OneNote. Links can also be a means of establishing associations between OneNote, OneNote pages, and resources outside OneNote. Rather than go to the trouble of opening a document in Word 2010 when you need it, you can link the document to OneNote and open the Word document simply by clicking the link.

Links help you integrate OneNote with your other work.

Linking to Other Places in OneNote

Create a link to another notebook, section, page, or note so you can click the link and instantly go elsewhere. Links offer a convenient way to go from place to place. They also present an opportunity to organize your notes. For example, you can create a page with links to other sections and pages. You can use this page like a table of contents to see where you store information and quickly go, by clicking, to where information is stored.

Links show as blue text and are underlined. When you move the pointer over a link to a different place in OneNote, a ScreenTip shows you the file path to the notebook or section, or in the case of pages and notes, the name of the page you will arrive on when you click the link.

After clicking a link, you can return to your original place by clicking the Back button on the Quick Access toolbar (or by pressing Alt+Left Arrow).

Linking to Another Notebook, Section, or Page

The easiest way to link to another place in OneNote is to right-click the name of the notebook, section, or page where you want the link to go and choose Copy Link To on the shortcut menu. Then paste the link into a note. For example, to link to a section, right-click the section's name on the Navigation bar or section tabs, choose Copy Link to Section, and then click in a note and press Ctrl+V to paste the link.

You can also link to another location by selecting text for the link and clicking the Link button on the Insert tab. In the Link dialog box, select a notebook, section, or page as the link target and click OK. The advantage of this method is being able to select the text that forms the link.

OneNote offers a shortcut command for linking to a page in the currently open notebook: Type two left square brackets ([[), the page's name, and two right square brackets (]]). For example, typing [[Compounds]] creates a link named "Compounds"; clicking this link opens the Compounds page.

Linking to Another Note

To link to another note, right-click the note and then choose Copy Link to Paragraph. Then click in the note where you want the link to appear and paste the link by pressing Ctrl+V or clicking the Paste button on the Home tab.

In notes with more than one paragraph, the paragraph you right-click when you choose Copy Link to Paragraph is used as the text for the link.

Link to a Notebook, Section, or Page

(1) Right-click a section name in the Navigation bar or section tabs.

(2) Choose Copy Link to Section.

(3) Go to the page where you want to paste the link.

(4) Click in a note and press Ctrl+V.

(5) Select text for another link.

(6) Click the Insert tab.

(7) Click the Link button (or press Ctrl+K).

(8) In the Link dialog box, select a page as the link target and click OK.

(9) Type two left square brackets ([[), the name of a page in your notebook, and two right square brackets (]]) to create another page link.

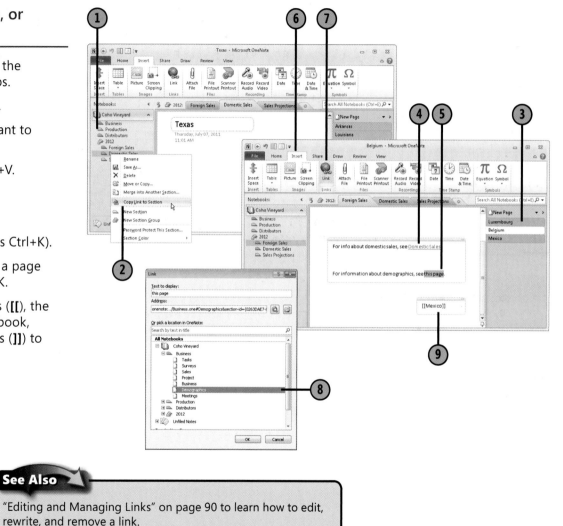

See Also

"Editing and Managing Links" on page 90 to learn how to edit, rewrite, and remove a link.

Link to Another Note

(1) Right-click the note that will be the target of the link.

(2) Choose Copy Link to Paragraph.

(3) Open a different page.

(4) Click on the page to create a new note.

(5) Click the Home tab.

(6) Click the Paste button to paste the link.

(7) Click the paragraph link you just created to activate the link.

(8) Click the Back button on the Quick Access toolbar to return to the page with the link.

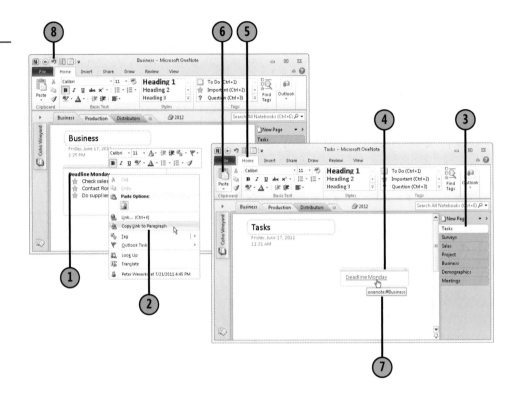

Creating Links to Web Pages and Files

Create a link to a web page so you can click the link and immediately open the web page in your browser. Being able to open web pages this way is convenient. Rather than open your browser and then go to a web page, you can simply click the link and go there straightaway.

Create a link to a file to be able to open a file by clicking its link. For example, clicking a link to a Word file opens the file in Word. File links are an opportunity for you to quickly refer to files or to trade information between notes and files.

You can tell where links are in notes because they show as blue text and are underlined. When you move the pointer over a link, a ScreenTip appears and the pointer turns into a hand. If the link is to a web page, the ScreenTip shows the link's web address; if the link is to a file, the ScreenTip shows the path to the file.

Creating Links to Web Pages

To create a link to a web page, you need to know the address of the web page to which the link will go. The easiest way to obtain this address is to go to the web page and copy the address from your browser's address bar. After you copy the address, you can paste it into the Link dialog box (the dialog box used to create links).

Start by selecting the text that will form the link. Then go to the Insert tab and click the Link button, right-click and choose Link, or press Ctrl+K. The Link dialog box opens. Enter the web address in the Address box with one of these techniques:

- Type the address.

- Paste the address (right-click and choose Paste) if you previously copied the address to the Clipboard.

- Click the Browse the Web button to open your browser. Then go to the web page, copy its address from your browser's address bar, return to the Link dialog box, and paste the address into the Address box (right-click and choose Paste).

Creating Links to Files

To create a file link, select the text that will form the link. Then press Ctrl+K, right-click and choose Link, or go to the Insert tab and click the Link button. In the Link dialog box, click the Browse for File button and select the target file in the Link to File dialog box.

Create a Link to a Web Page

1. Select the text that will form the link.

2. Click the Insert tab.

3. Click the Link button.

4. Click the Browse the Web button to open your browser.

5. In your browser, go to the web page.

6. Click the address bar.

7. Right-click and choose Copy.

8. In OneNote, right-click in the Address box and choose Paste.

9. Click OK.

10. Move the pointer over the link and notice the address in the ScreenTip.

See Also

"Placing Images in Notes" on page 68 to learn how to take a screen clipping, a picture of part of a web page, document, or other item on your computer screen.

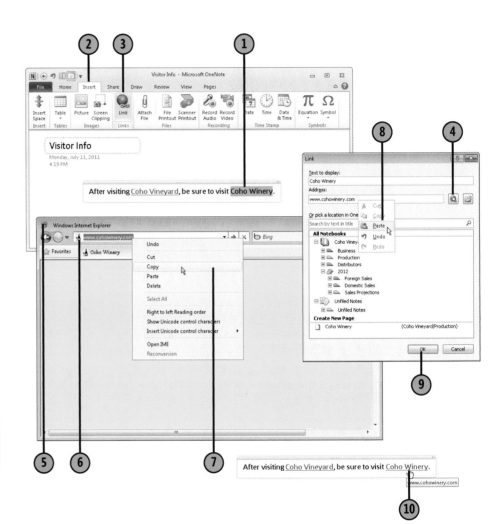

Create a Link to a File

① Select the text that will form the link.

② Click the Insert tab.

③ Click the Link button.

④ In the Link dialog box, click the Browse for File button.

⑤ In the Link to File dialog box, select a file and click OK.

⑥ Click OK in the Link dialog box.

⑦ Move the pointer over the link and notice the file path in the ScreenTip.

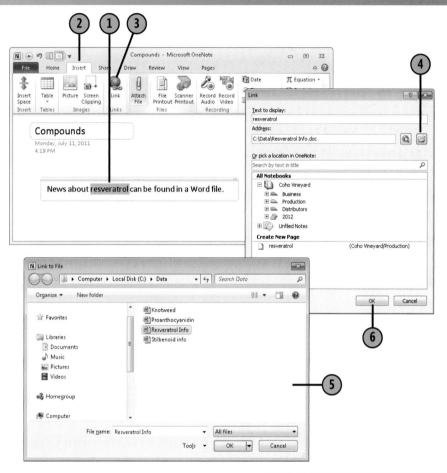

Tip

When you click a file link, the file opens in the default program. In Windows 7, you can choose default programs for different file types by clicking the Start button and choosing Default Programs. Click Set Your Default Programs to open the Default Programs window and establish default programs for your computer.

Caution

A file link is broken if the target file is deleted or moved. When you click a broken link, the Unable to Open File dialog box appears.

See Also

"Editing and Managing Links" on page 90 to learn how to edit, rewrite, and remove a link.

Editing and Managing Links

To edit or otherwise manage a link, start by right-clicking it. On the shortcut menu are commands for doing these tasks:

- Changing the link target: Choose Edit Link, and in the Link dialog box, change the address of the link (if the link is to a web page or file) or the location of a link (if the link is to another place in OneNote).

- Rewriting a link: Choose Edit Link, and in the Link dialog box, rewrite the text in the Text to Display box.

- Copying a link: Choose Copy Link. The link is copied to the Clipboard. You can paste it in a note.

- Selecting a link: Choose Select Link. Selecting is helpful when you want to format the link. With the link selected, you can choose text formatting commands.

- Removing a link: Choose Remove Link. The text remains, but the link is no longer live.

Edit and Manage a Link

① Right-click a link to a web page, file, or OneNote location.

② Choose Edit Link.

③ Rewrite the link text in the Text to Display box.

④ Choose a different location for the link.

⑤ Click OK.

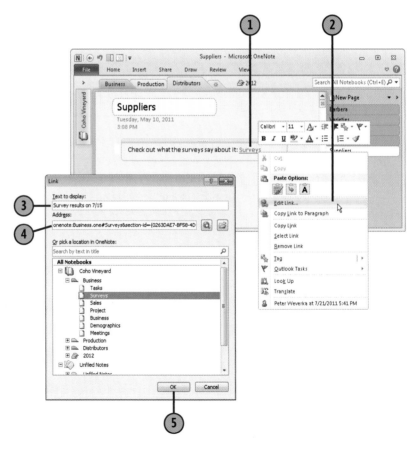

Taking Linked Notes

Linked notes are notes that are linked to a web page, Word document, PowerPoint 2010 presentation, or OneNote page. After you click the Link Notes button, OneNote automatically links the notes you take to the web page, Word document, PowerPoint presentation, or OneNote page that is open on your screen.

Taking linked notes is a convenient way to refer to an item you took notes about. All you have to do to open the item about which you took notes is click the Internet Explorer icon, Word icon, PowerPoint icon, or OneNote icon in the note. These icons appear to the left of paragraphs in linked notes.

Opening the Docked Window

OneNote provides a special docked window for taking linked notes. To open this window and begin taking linked notes, use one of these techniques:

- Starting in OneNote: On the Review tab, click the Linked Notes button. A second OneNote window opens and docks to the right side of the screen. Meanwhile, the Select Location in OneNote dialog box opens. Using this dialog box, select the page where you want to take linked notes. The page opens in the docked OneNote window.

- Starting in Word or PowerPoint: On the Review tab, click the Linked Notes button. A OneNote window opens and docks to the right side of the screen. Go to the Pages tab in this window, click Search, and select the page where you want to take linked notes about your Word document or PowerPoint presentation.

Taking Linked Notes in the Docked Window

On the left side of the screen, open and display a Word document, PowerPoint presentation, OneNote page, or web page (open the web page in Internet Explorer). Then, in the docked window, take notes as you normally would. OneNote creates the links as you take your notes. Links appear to the left of paragraphs in the form of Internet Explorer, Word, PowerPoint, and OneNote icons.

You can open and display a different web page, document, presentation, or OneNote page and then take notes about it. In the docked window, OneNote links your notes to whatever page, document, or presentation is active on the left side of the screen.

To open a different OneNote page in the docked window, display the ribbon (if necessary), click the Pages tab, click Search, and select a different page.

Handling Linked Notes in the Docked Window

Click the Linked Notes icon in the upper-left corner of the docked window to handle linked notes. Clicking this icon opens a menu with options for handling linked notes:

- Opening a linked item: Choose Linked File(s) to see a submenu with the names of all Word documents, PowerPoint presentations, web pages, and OneNote pages linked to the page that is open in the docked window. You can select an item on the submenu to open it on the left side of the screen. (You can also open a link by clicking its link icon.)

- Deleting links: Choose Delete Link(s) on This Page to see a submenu with the names of all links on the page. Select a link to delete it; select Delete All Links on This Page to delete all the links. (You can also delete a link by right-clicking its icon and choosing Remove Link.)

- Stopping and starting: Choose Stop Taking Linked Notes if you want OneNote to stop taking linked notes; choose Start Taking Linked Notes to resume taking linked notes.

- Choosing Linked Notes Options: Choose Linked Notes Options to open the OneNote Options dialog box and, under Linked Notes, choose options for handling linked notes.

Closing the Docked Window

When you finish taking linked notes in the docked window, click its Close button to close it. This button is located in the upper-right corner of the window.

Opening a Linked File

You can tell when a OneNote page has links to Word documents, PowerPoint presentations, web pages, or other OneNote pages because the Linked Notes icon appears in the upper-left corner of the page.

By clicking this icon and link icons on the left side of paragraphs, you can open files to which the page is linked.

Use these techniques to open a linked file:

- Click the Linked Notes icon, choose Linked Files, and select the name of a Word document, PowerPoint presentation, web page, or OneNote page on the submenu.

- Click the icon next to a note paragraph. (By hovering the pointer over this icon, you can see a document snippet or page thumbnail that suggests what the file is.)

Take Linked Notes

(1) In OneNote, open the page you want to take notes from.

(2) Click the Review tab.

(3) Click Linked Notes.

(4) In the Select Location in s, select the page where you want to take notes and click OK.

(5) In the docked OneNote window, write notes regarding the other OneNote window.

(6) Click the Linked Notes icon in the upper-left corner of the docked window.

(7) Choose Linked Files on the gallery.

(8) Read the list of files and web pages that are linked to the OneNote page in the docked window.

(9) Click the docked window's Close button to close the docked window.

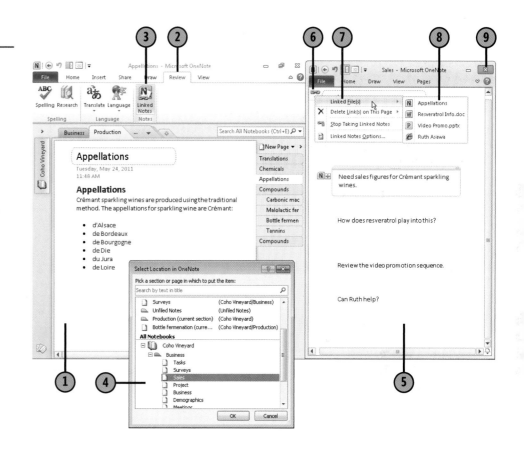

Caution

To take linked notes about a web page, you must open the web page in the Internet Explorer browser.

Open a Linked Notes Page or File

① Open a page with linked notes.

② Click the Linked Notes icon in the upper-left corner of the page and choose Linked File(s).

③ Read the list of files and pages linked to the OneNote page on the sub-menu (you can click a file on the list to open it).

④ Hover the pointer over notes to see which notes are linked to files (icons appear to the left of these notes).

⑤ Hover the pointer over an icon to see a document snippet or thumpage thumbnail that indicates what the file is.

⑥ Click an icon to open the file or page with which a note is linked.

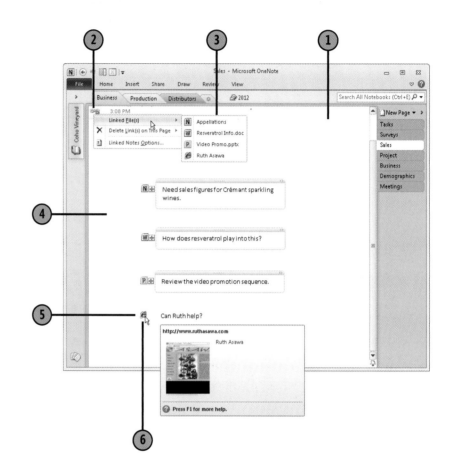

9

Making OneNote Easier to Use

Microsoft OneNote 2010 presents many opportunities for rearranging and changing the screen so you can get your work done faster and easier.

When you need more room in the page window to write and read notes, you can minimize the Navigation bar, pages tabs, and the ribbon. You can change views as well. OneNote 2010 offers Full Page view for reading notes and Normal view for organizing and formatting notes.

When you're taking notes from a web browser or application, consider docking OneNote to the desktop. Docking entails moving the OneNote screen to the right side of the monitor window so you can write notes and still see other applications.

To easily switch between different pages, open a second (or third or fourth) OneNote window. You can jump from window to window quickly by clicking the OneNote button on the Windows taskbar and making a page selection.

OneNote also offers the standard zoom-in and zoom-out commands to make reading easier. These commands are found on the View tab.

Handling the Navigation Bar and Page Tabs

Use the Navigation bar (on the left side of the screen) and page tabs (on the right side) to get from place to place in OneNote. In Normal view, the Navigation bar lists the names of open notebooks, and within each notebook are the names of sections and section groups. The page tabs show you the names of pages and subpages in the section you are viewing.

To make more room in the page window for writing and reading notes, you can collapse the Navigation bar and page tabs. And when you want to see the Navigation bar and page tabs again, you can expand them.

OneNote offers these techniques for handling the Navigation bar and page tabs:

- Dragging: Drag the border between the page window and Navigation bar or page tabs. To change the size this way, the Navigation bar and page tabs must be expanded (click the Expand Navigation Bar or Expand Page Tabs button).

- Clicking buttons: Click the Expand Navigation Bar or Collapse Navigation Bar button to expand or collapse the Navigation bar. Click the Expand Page Tabs or Collapse Page Tabs button to expand or collapse the page tabs.

- Pressing keyboard shortcuts: Press Ctrl+Shift+[to widen the page tabs; press Ctrl+Shift+] to narrow the page tabs. Keep pressing a keyboard shortcut until the page tabs are the size you want.

Collapse and Expand the Navigation Bar and Page Tabs

1. Move the pointer over the border between the Navigation bar and the page window, and when you see the double-headed arrow, drag the border to the right to widen the Navigation bar. (If you can't drag the border, click the Expand Navigation Bar button before completing this step.)

2. Click the Collapse Navigation Bar button.

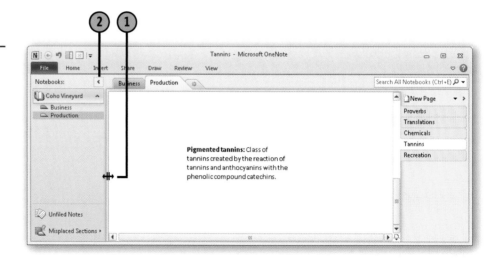

③ Click the Expand Navigation Bar button.

④ Move the pointer over the border between the page tabs and the page window, and when you see the double-headed arrow, drag the border to the left to widen the page tabs.

⑤ Press Ctrl+Shift+] several times to narrow the page tabs.

⑥ Click the Collapse Page Tabs button.

⑦ Click the Expand Page Tabs button.

See Also

Another way to collapse the Navigation bar and page tabs is to switch to Full Page view. See "Changing Screen Views" on page 100 to learn how to switch between Normal view and Full Page view.

Tip

To give yourself a lot of room for writing and reading notes, you can hide the Navigation bar. On the File tab, click Options, and in the Options dialog box, go to the Display area and clear the Navigation Bar Appears on Left check box.

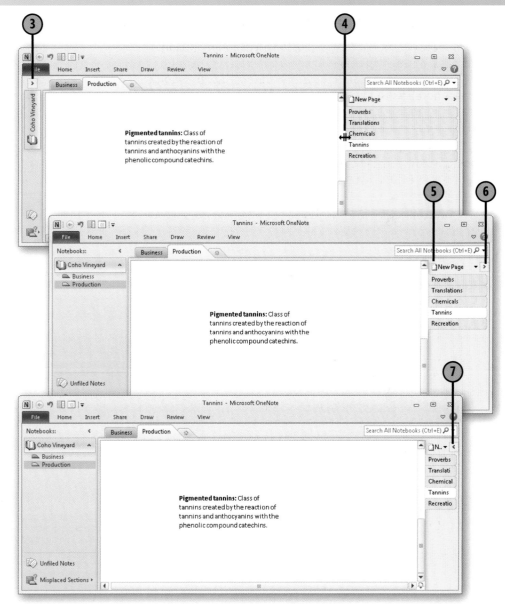

Minimizing and Expanding the Ribbon

The ribbon is the assortment of buttons and commands that appears along the top of the screen when you click a tab. When you need to focus on reading notes, consider minimizing the ribbon. With the ribbon minimized, there is more room for reading notes.

Use one of these techniques to minimize the ribbon:

- Click the Minimize the Ribbon button (this button is located in the upper-right corner of the screen).
- Press Ctrl+F1.
- Right-click the ribbon and select Minimize the Ribbon.
- Double-click a tab.

Use one of these techniques to expand the ribbon:

- Click the Expand the Ribbon button (located in the upper-right corner of the screen).
- Press Ctrl+F1.
- Right-click a tab on the ribbon and deselect Minimize the Ribbon.
- Double-click a tab.

When the ribbon is minimized, you can still access the buttons and other commands on a tab. To do so, move the pointer over a tab name and click it to expose the tab. After you perform an action on the tab, the ribbon minimizes itself.

Minimize and Expand the Ribbon

1. Click the Minimize the Ribbon button (if the ribbon is already minimized and you can't see this button, press Ctrl+F1).

2 Click the View tab and notice that the View tab and its buttons appear.

3 Click the Zoom In button and notice that the ribbon minimizes again after you use a command on the tab.

4 Double-click any tab to maximize the ribbon.

5 Right-click any tab and choose Minimize the Ribbon.

6 Click the Expand the Ribbon button.

See Also

"Customizing the Ribbon" on page 206 to learn how to customize the ribbon.

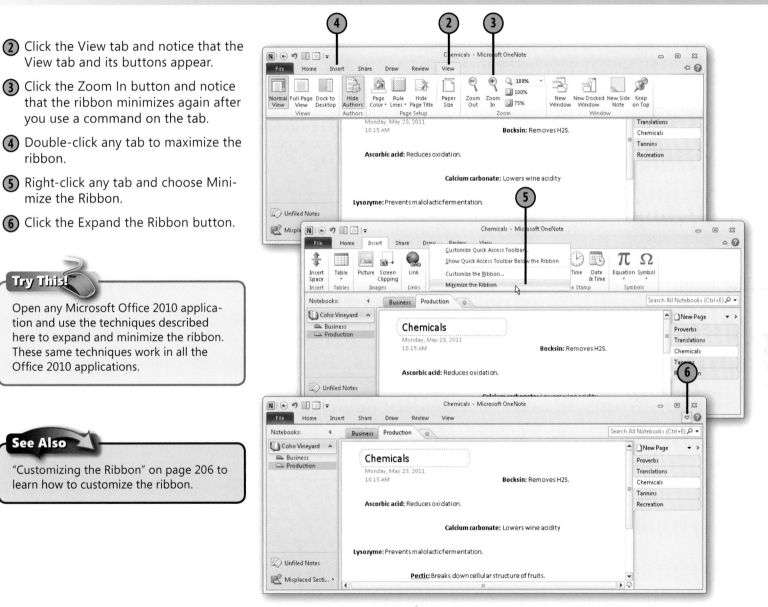

Changing Screen Views

OneNote offers two views of the screen. In Full Page view, the Navigation bar and page tabs do not appear. In Normal view, you can see the Navigation bar and page tabs. Normal view is for writing, editing, and organizing notes; Full Page view is for reading notes comfortably.

Use these techniques to switch between Full Page view and Normal view:

- Click the Full Page View button on the Quick Access toolbar or View tab.

Change Your View of the Screen

① Click the Full Page View button on the Quick Access toolbar to switch to Full Page view.

- Click the Normal View button on the View tab.

- Press F11.

In Full Page view, OneNote adds another tab, called Pages, to the ribbon. You can use the Pages tab to go from page to page, add pages, delete pages, and move pages. You can also search notebooks by clicking the Search button on the Pages tab.

2 Click the View tab.

3 Click the Normal View button to switch to Normal view.

4 Press F11 to switch to Full Page view.

5 Click the Full Page View button on the Quick Access toolbar to switch to Normal view (because the View buttons are toggles, clicking them a second time reverts to the previous view).

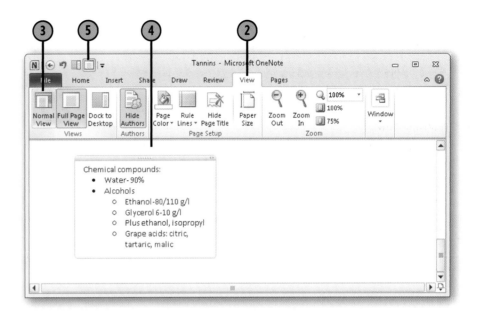

You can hide the Navigation bar and page tabs in Normal view as well as Full Screen view. See "Handling the Navigation Bar and Page Tabs" on page 96 to learn how to hide and display the Navigation bar and page tabs in Normal view.

Docking OneNote to the Desktop

Docking OneNote to the desktop means to shunt OneNote to the right side of the screen where it is out of the way but can still be used for taking and reading notes. Dock OneNote when you are taking notes from a browser window or document.

Use these techniques to dock and undock OneNote:

- Click the Dock to Desktop button on the Quick Access toolbar.

- Click the Dock to Desktop button on the View tab.
- Press Ctrl+Alt+D.

You can change the width of the OneNote screen after it is docked by dragging the left side. When docked, OneNote presents an abridged version of the ribbon with only four tabs: Home, Draw, View, and Pages.

Dock OneNote to the Desktop

(1) Click the Dock to Desktop button on the Quick Access toolbar to dock the OneNote screen.

(2) Move the pointer over the left side of the docked window; when you see the double-headed arrow, drag to the left or right to change the size of the docked OneNote window.

(3) Click the View tab.

(4) Click the Dock to Desktop button on the View tab to undock OneNote (the button is a toggle, and clicking it a second time reverses the previous action).

Tip

As well as opening a second (or third or fourth) OneNote window, you can open another docked window. On the View tab, click the New Docked Window button.

See Also

"Taking Linked Notes" on page 91 to learn how you can take notes in a docked One-Note window and have OneNote automatically link the notes you take to a web page, Microsoft Word document, Microsoft PowerPoint presentation, or OneNote page that is open on-screen.

Opening Another OneNote Window

Open another OneNote window when you want to examine notes on different pages and be able to jump back and forth between the pages. To open another window, click the New Window button on the View tab or press Ctrl+M. OneNote also offers the New Docked Window button on the View tab to open another window and dock it to the desktop.

To switch between open OneNote windows, click the OneNote button on the Windows taskbar, and on the pop-up menu, choose a page name. You can also press Alt+Tab and choose a window in the dialog box that appears.

Open Another OneNote Window

1. Click the View tab.

2. Click the New Window button to open a new window.

3. In the new window, click a different page in the page tab.

4. Click the OneNote button on the Windows taskbar to see a list of open OneNote windows.

5. On the list, click the name of the page in the first window you opened to return to the first window.

6. Click the first window's Close button to close the first window.

Tip
Click the Keep on Top button on the View tab to keep a One-Note window (or the OneNote window, if only one window is open) on top of all other open windows.

Tip
Click the New Docked Window button on the View tab to open a new window and dock the new window to the desktop.

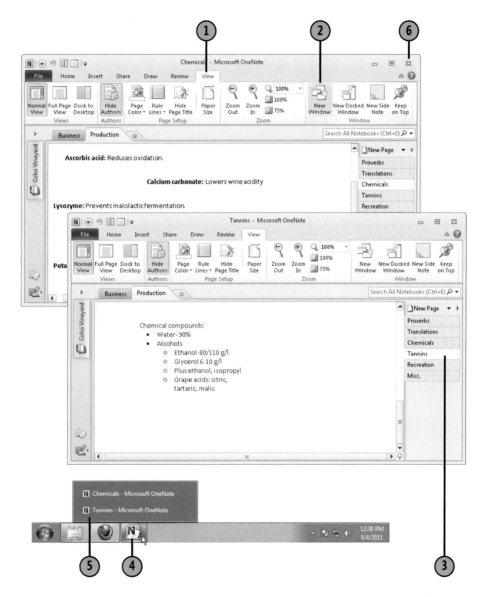

Zooming In and Out

OneNote offers a number of Zoom buttons and controls on the View tab. Use them to zoom in and out and get a better view of your work. Zoom in, for example, when drawing a note to draw with precision; zoom out to see more notes on the page.

OneNote offers these zoom methods:

- Zoom in: Click the Zoom In button on the View tab, press Alt+Ctrl+plus key (the plus key on the keypad), or press Alt+Ctrl+Shift+plus key.

- Zoom out: Click the Zoom Out button on the View tab, press Alt+Ctrl+minus key (the minus key on the keypad), or press Alt+Ctrl+Shift+minus key.

- Zoom by percentage: On the View tab, make a choice on the Zoom menu or enter a percentage, click the 100% button, or click the 75% button.

Zoom In and Out

1. Click the View tab.

2. Open the Zoom menu and choose 50%.

3. Click the 75% button.

4. Click the Zoom In button twice.

5. Enter 250 in the Zoom menu and press Enter.

6. Click the 100 percent button.

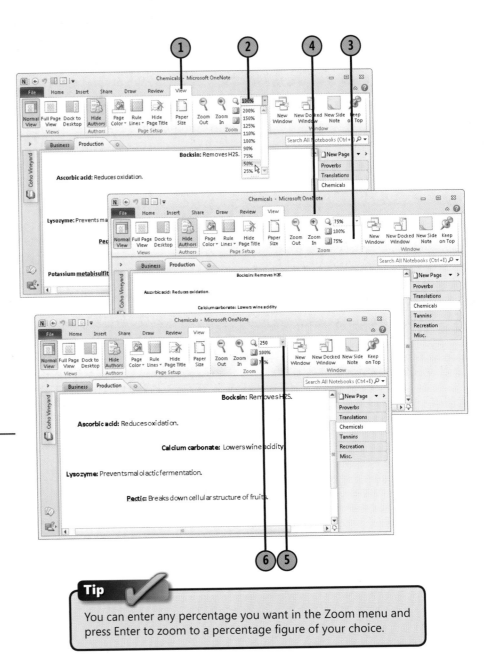

Tip

You can enter any percentage you want in the Zoom menu and press Enter to zoom to a percentage figure of your choice.

10

Spell Checking Your Notes

If you intend to share notes with others, be sure to spell check your notes to fix all misspellings. Microsoft OneNote 2010 offers a couple of different ways to spell check notes. You can correct misspellings one at a time or run a spell checker to review and correct all the misspellings on a page.

If your notes include foreign language words, you can spell check them as well. OneNote 2010 also offers the AutoCorrect feature for correcting misspellings as you make them. You can add your own words to the list of words that are autocorrected. For that matter, you can trick the AutoCorrect feature into entering difficult-to-type words for you.

Running a Spell Check

Unless you opted to hide spelling errors in notes, you can tell where spelling errors are because they are underlined in red. To fix spelling errors, you can either right-click misspelled words and correct them one at a time or run a spell check.

When spell checking, OneNote occasionally flags a word that is correctly spelled. You can ignore these words or add them to the spelling dictionary. Adding a word to the spelling dictionary tells OneNote that the word is legitimate and should no longer be considered a misspelling.

Correct Misspellings One at a Time

① Write the following sentence in a note (including the misspelled *frient*): **His frient Mr. Hayford lives in Geyserville**.

② Right-click the misspelled *frient* and choose friend, the correct spelling, on the shortcut menu.

③ Right-click the name *Hayford* and choose Ignore (ignore this presumed misspelling because Hayford is a correctly spelled name).

④ Right-click the city name *Geyserville* and choose Add to Dictionary (so that this city's name is added to the dictionary and is not considered a misspelling anymore).

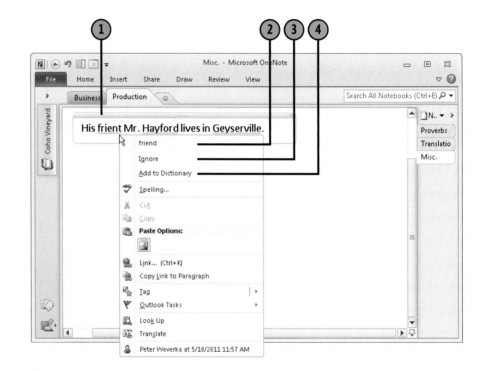

See Also

"Customizing the Spell Checker" on page 110 to learn how to hide or display the wavy red underlines that mark misspelled words.

Run a Spell Check

(1) Write the following sentence in a note (including the misspelled *silter* and the duplicate word *lives*): **His silter Mrs. Longsford lives lives in Connorsville.**

(2) Click the Review tab.

(3) Click the Spelling button (or press F7).

(4) In the Spelling task pane, select the word *sister* in the Suggestions list and click the Change button to enter the correct word, sister, in the sentence.

(5) Click the Ignore button to ignore the presumed misspelling *Longford* (it is a correctly spelled name).

(6) Click the Delete button to delete the second *lives* from the sentence (the Delete button appears in the Spelling task pane when the spell checker encounters duplicate words).

(7) Click the Add to Dictionary button to add the city name *Connorsville* to the dictionary (this name will no longer be considered a misspelling).

(8) Click the Close button to close the Spelling task pane.

Tip ✓

You can run a spell check without going first to the Review tab and clicking the Spelling button. Just press F7.

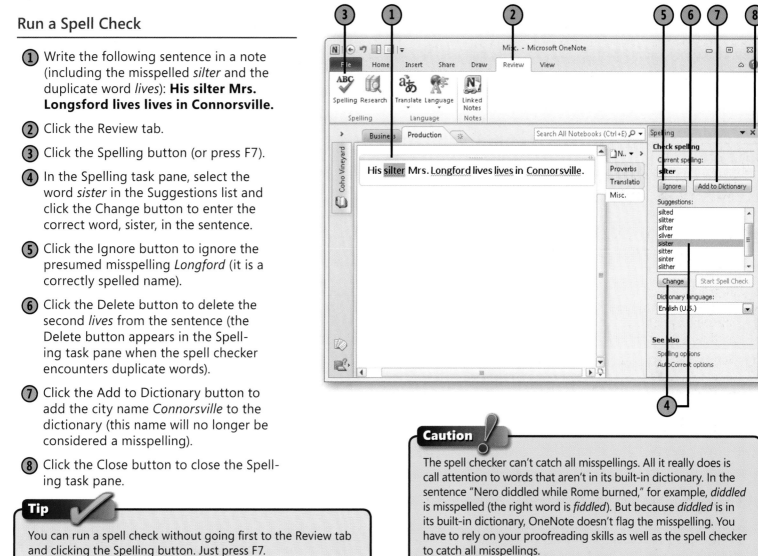

Caution ❗

The spell checker can't catch all misspellings. All it really does is call attention to words that aren't in its built-in dictionary. In the sentence "Nero diddled while Rome burned," for example, *diddled* is misspelled (the right word is *fiddled*). But because *diddled* is in its built-in dictionary, OneNote doesn't flag the misspelling. You have to rely on your proofreading skills as well as the spell checker to catch all misspellings.

Customizing the Spell Checker

Customize the spell checker to make it run more to your liking. OneNote offers many ways to customize the spell checker. For example, you can turn off the wavy red lines that appear under misspelled words and choose whether to spell check uppercase words.

OneNote Spell Checking Options

Option	Description
Ignore words in UPPERCASE	Doesn't spell check any uppercase words on the presumption that they are acronyms.
Ignore words that contain numbers	Doesn't spell check words containing numbers.
Ignore Internet and file addresses	Doesn't spell check URLs and file addresses (words with at symbols, @, and slashes, /).
Flag repeated words	Flags duplicate words in spell checks.
Enforce accented uppercase in French	Flags uppercase letters in French words that should be accented (French Canadian retains accents in uppercase words but standard French doesn't).
Suggest from main dictionary only	For spelling corrections, suggests words from the built-in dictionary, not dictionaries that you create or install.
Custom Dictionaries	Click this button to open the Custom Dictionaries dialog box, in which you can edit the built-in dictionary (Custom.dic), choose the default dictionary for spell checks, create a dictionary, and install a dictionary.
French modes	For spell checking French words, determines how to handle traditional and new spellings.
Spanish modes	For spell checking Spanish words, determines how to handle Tuteo and Voseo verb forms.
Check spelling as you type	Checks for misspellings as you type words.
Hide spelling errors	Hides or displays the wavy red lines that appear under misspellings.

Customize the Spell Checker

(1) Press F7 to open the Spelling task pane.

(2) Click the Spelling Options link (it's located at the bottom of the Spelling task pane).

(3) Choose options in the OneNote Options dialog box.

(4) Click OK.

Caution

Options you choose in the OneNote Options dialog box apply to spell checking in all Microsoft Office 2010 applications, not just OneNote 2010.

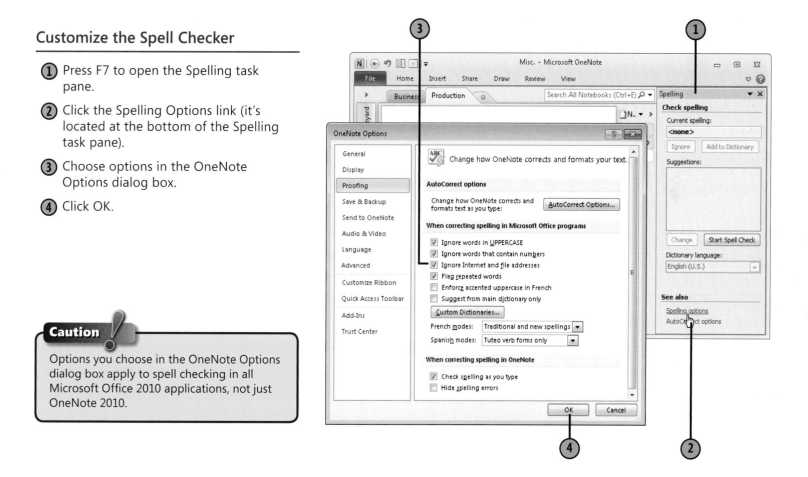

Spell Checking Foreign-Language Text

Besides spell checking English text, you can spell check text in other languages. Versions of Office 2010 available in North America come with an English, French, and Spanish dictionary for spell checking purposes. To spell check text in a language apart from English, French, or Spanish, download and install its dictionary starting at this web page: http://office.microsoft.com/en-us/language/.

To spell check text in a foreign language, you first identify to OneNote what the language is. Then you run a spell check the usual way.

Spell Check Foreign Language Text

1. Write the following Spanish sentence in a note (including the misspelled *est*): **Susana est en la casa.**

2. Drag to select the sentence.

3. Click the Review tab.

4. Click the Language button and choose Set Proofing Language on the drop-down menu.

5. In the Proofing Language taskbar, select a Spanish option.

6. Right-click the misspelled *est* (it is underlined in red) and choose esta, the correct spelling, on the shortcut menu.

> **See Also**
>
> "Translating Text" on page 170 to learn how to translate text to and from different languages.

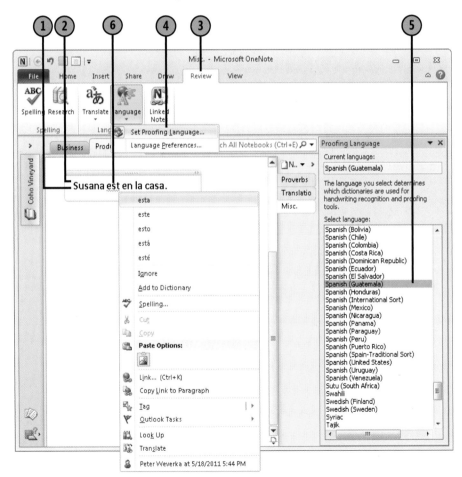

Correcting Common Misspellings

OneNote (and all the other Office 2010 applications) have a built-in AutoCorrect feature that corrects misspellings automatically. For example, if you mistype the word *only* by typing *onyl*, OneNote corrects the misspelling as soon as you make it. Right after you type *onyl* and press the Spacebar, OneNote corrects you and you see the word only.

You can use AutoCorrect to do more than automatically correct misspellings. You can also use it to enter hard-to-type jargon, scientific terms, and the like.

Autocorrect Common Misspellings

(1) In a note, type the following misspelling of the word *accident* and press the Spacebar to see how AutoCorrect fixes misspellings: **accidant**.

(2) Press F7 to open the Spelling task pane.

(3) Click the AutoCorrect Options link (it's located at the bottom of the Spelling task pane).

(4) In the AutoCorrect dialog box, scroll through the Replace-With word pairs to accidant-accident to see some of the words that AutoCorrect fixes automatically.

(5) In the Replace box, enter the following: **/cs**.

(6) In the With box, enter the following: **Cordyceps sinensis** (this is the name of a mushroom species).

(7) Click Add.

(8) Click OK.

(9) In a note, enter **/cs** and press the Spacebar to see how you can use AutoCorrect to enter a hard-to-type scientific term; in this case, Cordyceps sinensis.

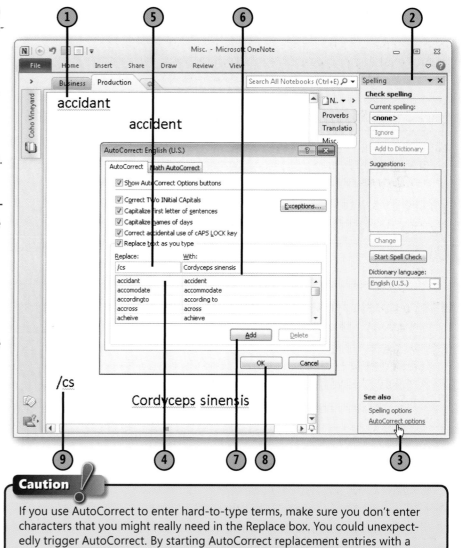

Caution

If you use AutoCorrect to enter hard-to-type terms, make sure you don't enter characters that you might really need in the Replace box. You could unexpectedly trigger AutoCorrect. By starting AutoCorrect replacement entries with a slash (/), you make it less likely to trigger AutoCorrect unexpectedly.

11

Drawing Notes

Sometimes saying it with pictures is better than saying it with words, and for those occasions, OneNote offers the Drawing tab. This tab presents tools for drawing free-form, drawing lines, and drawing shapes.

After you make a drawing, you can move it and change its size. You can also erase parts of it. The Drawing tab also has tools for rotating drawings and determining how drawings overlap when more than one occupies the same space on a page.

Drawing is easiest if you have a tablet PC or pen device, but you can also draw by dragging the mouse. When you draw, you can choose between lines of various widths, colors, and transparencies.

Drawing Free-Form with a Pen or Highlighter

To draw free-form or handwrite a note, go to the Draw tab, select a pen or highlighter in the Pens gallery, and drag your pen device or mouse on the page. After you finish drawing or handwriting, click the Select & Type button on the Drawing tab to tell OneNote that you want to resume typing notes, not drawing them.

The difference between pens and highlighters is that lines you draw with a highlighter are transparent.

Draw Free-Form with a Pen or Highlighter

1. Click the Draw tab.

2. Select a pen or highlighter in the Pens gallery.

3. Drag with a pen device or mouse on the page to draw a free-form line.

4. Click the More button in the Pens gallery (this button is located below the Pens gallery scroll bar).

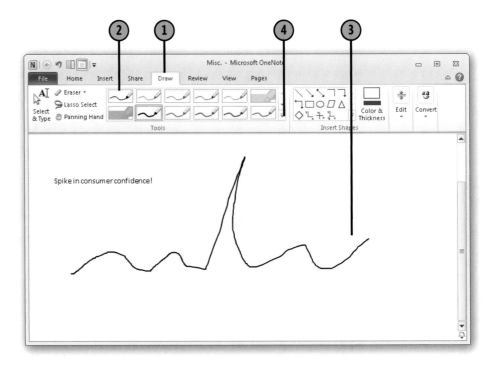

⑤ Select a built-in pen.

⑥ Drag on the page to draw a free-form line.

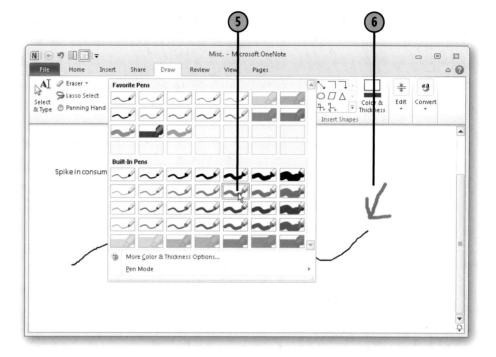

See Also

"Drawing Lines, Shapes, and Graphs" on page 120 to learn how to draw straight lines.

Caution

You can't draw if OneNote is in Create Handwriting Only mode. To see which mode OneNote is in, open the Pens gallery, select Pen Mode, and notice which option is selected on the Pen Mode menu. To be able to draw, Create Both Handwriting and Drawings mode or Creating Drawings Only mode must be selected.

See Also

"Handwriting Notes and Converting Them to Text" on page 61 to learn how to handwrite notes with a pen device or the mouse.

Creating a Free-Form Pen or Highlighter

OneNote offers options for creating pens and highlighters in the color and width of your choice. After you create a pen or highlighter, it is added to the Favorite Pens list. This list comprises pens and highlighters that are available at the top of the Pens gallery.

To create a pen or highlighter, click More in the Pens gallery and choose More Color & Thickness Options. Then, in the Pen Properties dialog box, select Pen or Highlighter, choose a thickness, and choose a color.

Pens and highlighters you create are added automatically to the Favorite Pens list. By right-clicking a pen or highlighter in this list, you can remove it, move it higher in the list, or move it lower in the list.

Create a Free-Form Pen or Highlighter

1. Click the Draw tab.
2. Click More in the Pens gallery.
3. Choose More Color & Thickness Options.
4. In the Pen Properties dialog box, choose Pen or Highlighter.
5. Choose a Thickness option.
6. Choose a Line Color option.
7. Click OK.

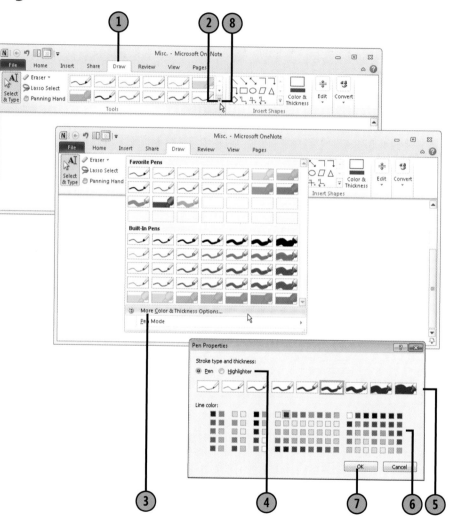

(8) Click More in the Pens gallery.

(9) Right-click the pen or highlighter you created and choose Move Up to move it higher in the Pens gallery and make it easier to find and select.

(10) Right-click the pen or highlighter you created and choose Remove Pen from This List.

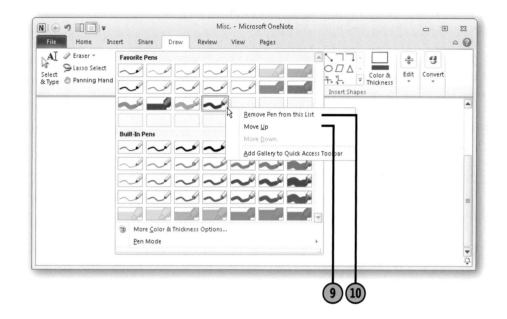

Drawing Lines, Shapes, and Graphs

Besides drawing free-form lines starting on the Draw tab, you can draw straight lines, shapes, and graphs:

- Straight lines: Draw lines, lines with arrows, and lines at 90-degree angles.

- Shapes: Draw rectangles, ovals, parallelograms, triangles, and diamonds.

- Graphs: Draw two- and three-dimensional graphs.

To draw a line, shape, or graph, start by clicking the Color & Thickness button and choosing a line thickness and color in the Color & Thickness dialog box. Then select a line, shape, or graph in the Insert Shapes gallery and drag on the page with a pen device or the mouse.

Draw Lines, Shapes, and Graphs

1. Click the Draw tab.

2. Click the Color & Thickness button.

3. In the Color & Thickness dialog box, choose Pen or Highlighter.

4. Choose a Thickness option.

5. Choose a Line Color option.

6. Click OK.

7. In the Insert Shapes gallery, click More.

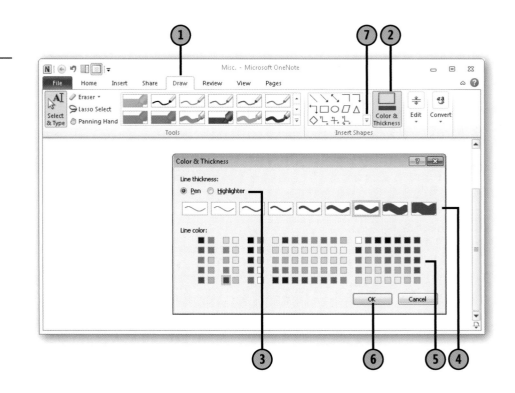

(8) Choose a line, shape, or graph.

(9) Drag with a pen device or mouse on the page to draw the line, shape, or graph.

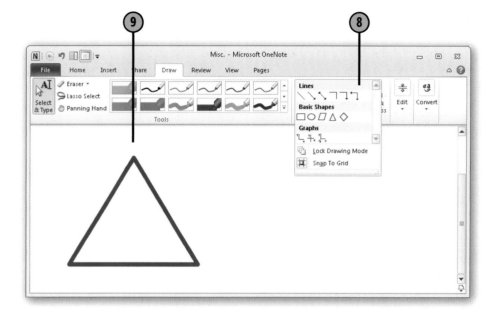

Tip

To change the thickness and color of a free-form line, line, or shape, select it, click the Color & Thickness button, and choose a different thickness and line color in the Color & Thickness dialog box.

See Also

"Manipulating Lines and Shapes" on page 124 to learn how to move and change the size of lines, shapes, and graphs.

Tip

To draw several instances of the same type of line, shape, or graph, choose Lock Drawing Mode in the Insert Shapes gallery before you start drawing. In Lock Drawing mode, OneNote creates the same type of shape when you draw. You don't have to return to the Insert Shapes gallery each time you want to start drawing a shape.

Using the Eraser

Use the Eraser on the Draw tab to erase all or parts of a free-form line, line, shape, or graph. OneNote offers two types of erasers:

- Eraser (small, medium, and large): Drag with this eraser over a line to erase part of a line.

- Stroke eraser: Click a line with this eraser to erase an entire line.

By erasing parts of lines, you can create new shapes. For example, by erasing part of an oval, you can create an arc.

Press Esc or click the Select & Type button when you finish erasing.

Use the Eraser

1. Click the Draw tab.

2. Open the gallery on the Eraser button and choose Medium eraser.

3. Drag across a line or shape to erase part of it.

4. Open the gallery on the Eraser button and choose Stroke Eraser.

5. Click a line to erase it.

6. Click the Select & Type button.

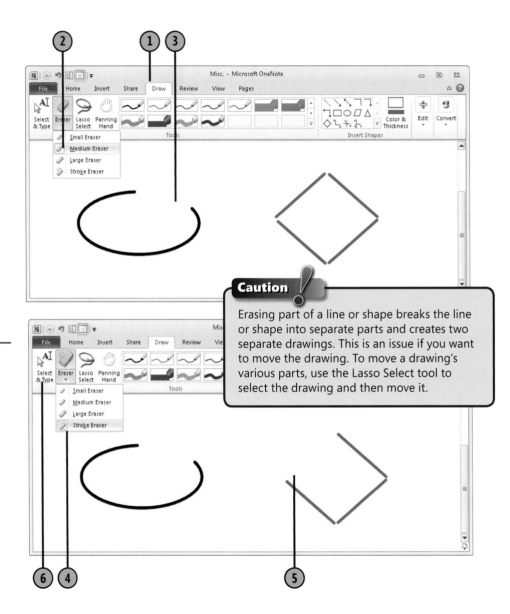

Caution

Erasing part of a line or shape breaks the line or shape into separate parts and creates two separate drawings. This is an issue if you want to move the drawing. To move a drawing's various parts, use the Lasso Select tool to select the drawing and then move it.

Panning to See Your Work

On a page that is crowded with many lines and shapes, it can be hard to find the line or shape you are looking for. For this reason, the Draw tab offers the Panning Hand.

Click the Panning Hand button on the Draw tab and drag horizontally to move the page from side to side, or drag vertically to move the page up or down.

Pan Across or Down the Page

① Click the Draw tab.

② Click the Panning Hand button.

③ Drag the page to the left.

④ Drag the page to the right.

⑤ Click Select & Type (or press Esc).

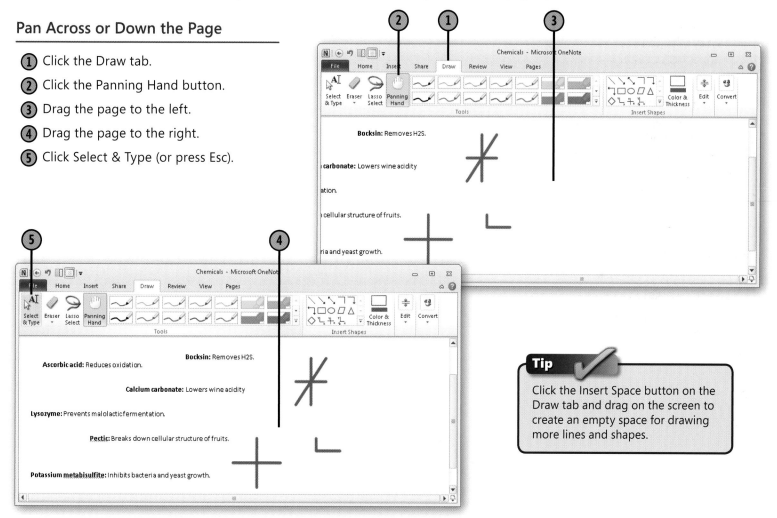

Tip

Click the Insert Space button on the Draw tab and drag on the screen to create an empty space for drawing more lines and shapes.

Manipulating Lines and Shapes

OneNote offers a handful of techniques for manipulating lines and shapes.

To select a line or shape, use one of these techniques:

- Move the pointer over a line or a line in a shape and double-click. For this method to work, the Select & Type button on the Draw tab must be selected. Use this technique to select one line or shape.

- Click the Lasso Select button on the Draw tab and drag around the lines or shapes you want to select. Use this technique to select one or more lines and shapes.

- Drag slantwise across the lines and shapes. Use this technique to select one or more lines and shapes.

To move a line or shape, select it. Then move the pointer over it and drag when the pointer turns into a four-headed arrow.

To change the size of a line or shape, follow these steps:

1 Select the line or shape.

2 Drag a handle.

- Shape: Drag a corner handle to change the shape's size but keep its proportions; drag a handle on the top, bottom, or side to change the size as well as the proportions.

- Line: Drag a handle.

To delete a line or shape, select it. Then press Delete or click the Delete button on the Draw tab.

Select Lines and Shapes

① Click the Draw tab.

② Click the Select & Type button.

③ Move the pointer directly over a line or a line in a shape and then double-click.

④ Click the Lasso Select button.

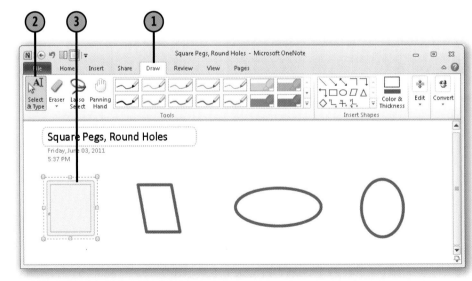

⑤ Drag around several objects and release the mouse button.

⑥ Click the Select & Type button (or press Esc).

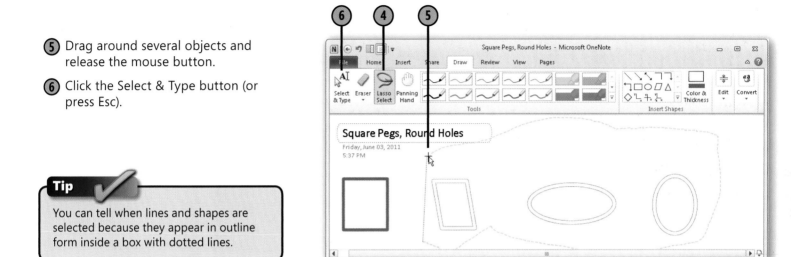

Move Lines and Shapes

(1) Click the Draw tab.

(2) Select the line or shape.

(3) Move the pointer over the line or shape so you can see the four-arrow pointer.

(4) Drag the line or shape to a different location.

(5) Drag slantwise across more than one line or shape to select the lines or shapes.

(6) Move the pointer over the items you selected so you can see the four-arrow pointer.

(7) Drag to move all the items to a different location.

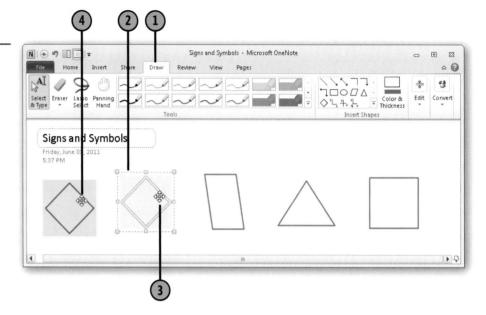

Tip

You can also move lines and shapes with the cut-and-paste method. Select the line or shape, right-click, and choose Cut; then right-click where you want to move the line or shape and choose a Paste command.

Tip

To help you line up shapes and note containers on pages, OneNote automatically snaps these items to an invisible grid. If you prefer that items not snap to this grid, click More on the Insert Shapes gallery and clear the Snap to Grid option. You can also press Alt as you drag items to temporarily turn the grid option off.

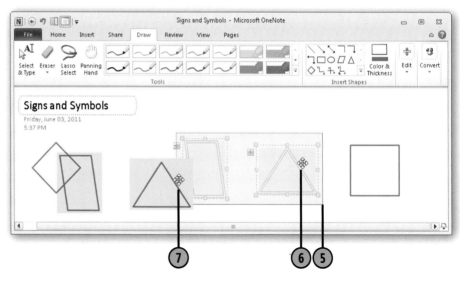

Resize Lines and Shapes

(1) Click the Draw tab.

(2) Select a shape.

(3) Move the pointer over a corner handle, and when you see the double-arrow pointer, drag to change the shape's size but keep its proportions.

(4) Select another shape.

(5) Move the pointer over a top, bottom, or side handle; when you see the double-arrow pointer, drag to change the shape's size and its proportions.

Delete Lines and Shapes

(1) Click the Draw tab.

(2) Select a line or shape.

(3) Click the Delete button (or press Delete).

See Also

"Using the Eraser" on page 122 to learn how to erase lines and shapes with the Eraser tool.

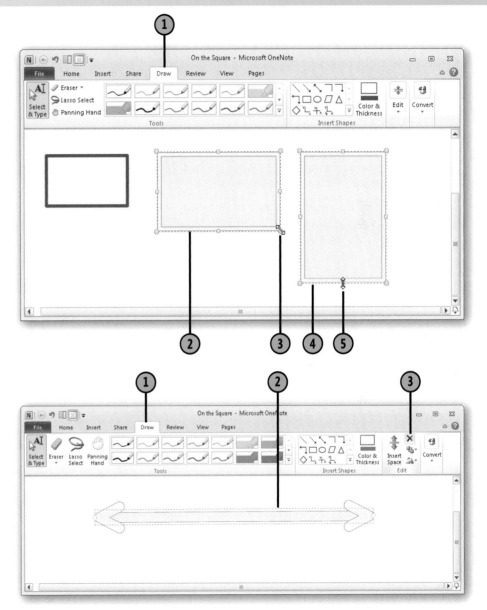

Arranging Overlapping Lines, Shapes, and Containers

When lines, shapes, and note containers overlap, you can determine which is on top by using an Arrange command on the Draw tab. Start by selecting the line, shape, or note container that you want to move up or down in a stack of overlapping items. Then, on the Draw tab, click the Arrange button and choose an option on the gallery:

- Bring Forward: Raises the item one layer in the stack.

- Bring to Front: Moves the item to the top of the stack.

- Send Backward: Lowers the item by one layer in the stack.

- Send to Back: Moves the item to the bottom of the stack.

Sometimes you have to repeat the Arrange command until the line or shape is where you want it to be in the stack.

Arrange Overlapping Lines, Shapes, and Containers

1. Click the Draw tab.

2. Click the Select & Type button.

3. Select a line, shape, or note container in a stack of items.

4. Click the Arrange button and choose Send to Back.

5. Click the Arrange button and choose Bring Forward.

6. Click the Arrange button and choose Send Backward.

7. Click the Arrange button and choose Bring to Front.

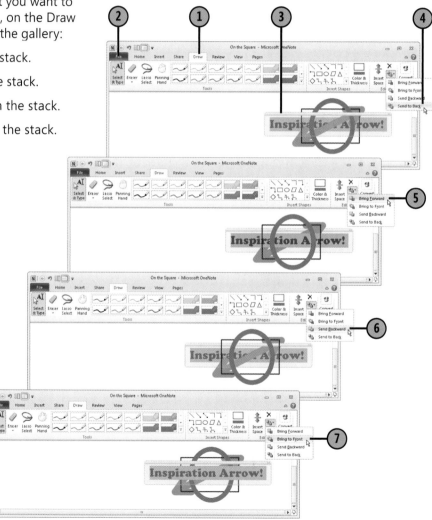

Rotating and Flipping Lines and Shapes

To rotate or flip a line or shape, start by selecting it. Then, on the Draw tab, click the Rotate button and choose an option in the gallery.

OneNote offers commands for flipping items and for rotating items to the left or right by 45 and 90 degrees.

Rotate and Flip Lines and Shapes

① Click the Draw tab.

② Select a line or shape.

③ Click the Rotate button and choose Rotate Right 90°.

④ Click the Rotate button and choose Flip Horizontal.

Tip ✓

You can also rotate a line by dragging its selection handle.

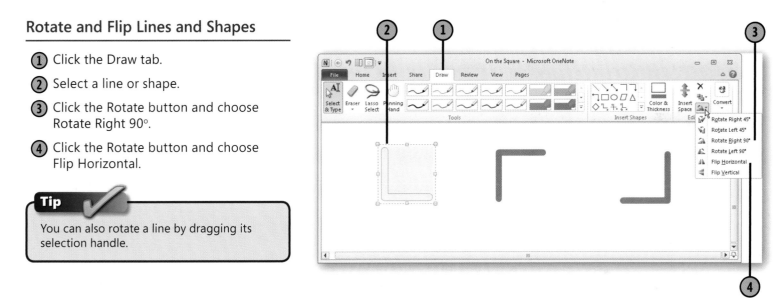

12

Organizing Your Notes

The more notes you take, the harder it is to stay organized. Notes that should be on one page end up on another. Sometimes pages need to be moved to a different section, and sections need to be moved to a different notebook.

OneNote offers commands for moving and copying pages and sections to different places.

One way to stay organized and be able to locate notes is to tag them. For example, you can tag notes that require a follow-up with the Important tag. When you need to find these notes, you can run the Find Tags command. OneNote comes with a selection of readymade tags, and you can create customized tags for your needs.

To help identify sections and pages, you can color-code them. Devise a color scheme for assigning colors to different topics and then color-code your notebooks, sections, and pages accordingly.

Moving, Copying, and Merging Pages and Sections

No matter how carefully you organize your notebooks and sections, you inevitably have to move or copy pages and sections to different places. OneNote offers these methods of moving and copying pages and sections:

- Move or copy pages to a different section: Use the Move or Copy command (or press Ctrl+Alt+M) to move or copy an individual page or several pages in a section to a different section. Right-click a page name on the page tabs to access the Move or Copy command.

Move or Copy a Page or Pages

1. In the page tabs, click the name of the page you want to move.

2. Right-click the page name and choose Move or Copy on the shortcut menu.

3. In the Move or Copy Pages dialog box, select the section where you want to move or copy the page.

4. Click the Move button.

- Move and copy all the pages in a section to a different section (merging): Use the Merge into Another Section command to move or copy all the pages in a section to a different section. Right-click a section name in the Navigation bar or section tabs to access the Merge into Another Section command.

- Move or copy a section to a different section group or notebook: Use the Move or Copy command to move or copy a section to another notebook or a different place in the same notebook. Right-click a section name in the Navigation bar or section tabs to access the Move or Copy command.

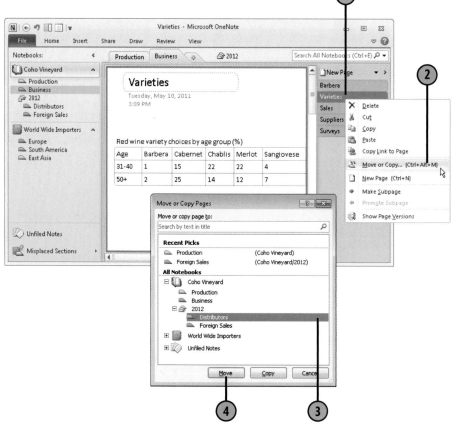

⑤ In the page tabs, Ctrl+click to select more than one page name.

⑥ Right-click one of the page names you selected and choose Move or Copy on the shortcut menu.

⑦ In the Move or Copy Pages dialog box, select the section where you want to move or copy the pages.

⑧ Click the Copy button.

⑨ Press Ctrl+Z (or click the Undo button) to undo the copy.

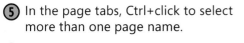

Merge (Move or Copy) All Pages in a Section

(1) In the Navigation bar or section tabs, right-click the section with the pages you want to merge with another section.

(2) Choose Merge into Another Section on the shortcut menu.

(3) In the Merge Section dialog box, select a section.

(4) Click the Merge button.

(5) In the Are You Sure? dialog box, click the Merge Sections button.

(6) In the Merge Was Successful dialog box, click the Delete button to delete the section with the pages that are now merged with the section you selected.

Tip ✓

Click No in the Merge Was Successful dialog box if you want to retain a copy of a section after you merge its pages with another section.

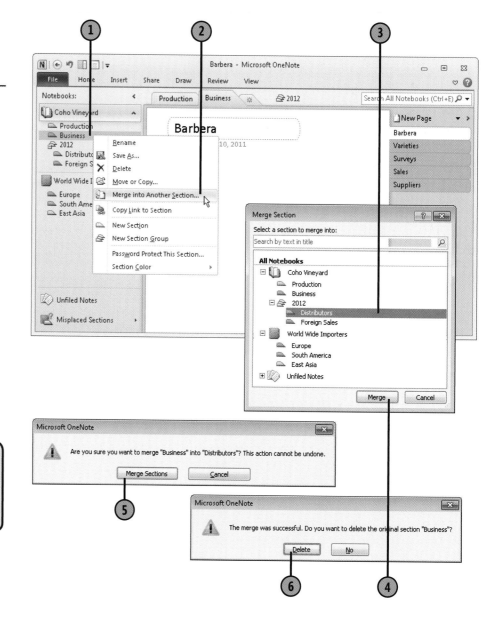

Move or Copy a Section to a Different Location

(1) In the Navigation bar or section tabs, right-click the section that you want to move or copy.

(2) Choose Move or Copy on the shortcut menu.

(3) In the Move or Copy Section dialog box, select a notebook or a section in the notebook that is currently open.

(4) Click the Move button (click the Copy button to copy the section).

Tip ✓

You can also move or copy a section by dragging its name higher or lower in the Navigation bar. To copy a section, hold down the Ctrl key as you drag the section name.

Tagging Notes for Follow Up

To make sure you follow up with notes, consider tagging them. Tagging a note means to mark it with an icon. Use the To Do tag, for example, to mark a note that lists tasks. Tagging enables you to quickly find notes. Moreover, you can use the Find Tags command to search for notes that you tagged.

Besides tagging notes, you can also tag page titles. You can also tag paragraphs in notes and assign more than one tag to the same note.

OneNote offers two dozen tags (To Do, Important, and others) in the Tags gallery on the Home tab. Some of the tags highlight notes rather than mark notes with icons. Some tags change the font color of notes. You can create tags to supplement the tags in the Tags gallery.

To tag, start by clicking the note, paragraph in a note, or page title that you want to tag. Then use one of these techniques:

- Open the Tags gallery on the Home tab and select a tag (the Tags gallery is located to the right of the Styles gallery).

- Right-click, choose Tag on the shortcut menu, and select a tag on the submenu.

To remove a tag, right-click it and choose Remove Tag on the shortcut menu (or choose Remove Tag in the Tags gallery).

Tag a Note or Page

① Click the note you want to tag; to tag a page, click its title box.

② Click the Home tab.

③ Click More on the Tags gallery to open this gallery (this button is located below the scroll bar).

④ Select a tag.

Tip ✔

The first eight tags in the Tags gallery are assigned the keyboard shortcuts Ctrl+1 through Ctrl+8. Press one of these keyboard shortcuts to assign a tag listed at the top of the Tags gallery.

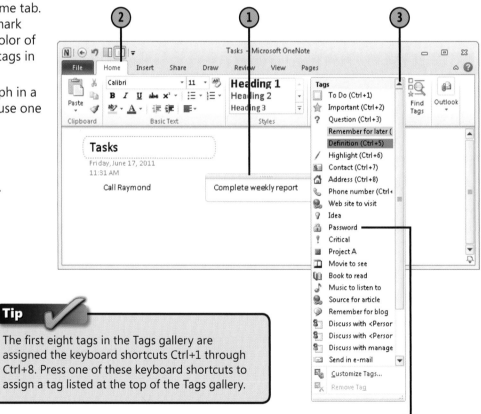

⑤ Right-click a paragraph in a note.

⑥ Choose Tag on the shortcut menu.

⑦ Select a tag on the Tag submenu.

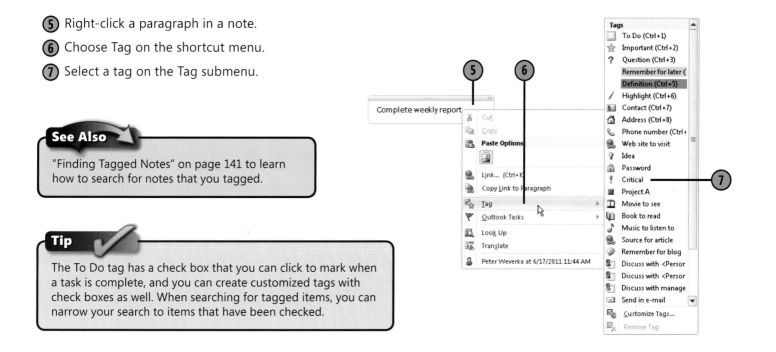

See Also

"Finding Tagged Notes" on page 141 to learn how to search for notes that you tagged.

Tip

The To Do tag has a check box that you can click to mark when a task is complete, and you can create customized tags with check boxes as well. When searching for tagged items, you can narrow your search to items that have been checked.

Remove a Tag

① Right-click the note you want to untag.

② Choose Remove Tag on the shortcut menu.

Tip

You can also remove a tag with these techniques:

- Press Ctrl+0 (the zero). To remove the tags from several notes, select them and press Ctrl+0.

- Open the Tags gallery and choose the Remove tag (the last option in the gallery).

- Select the tag on the Tags menu or shortcut menu. Each tag is a toggle, so selecting it a second time removes it.

Customizing Tags

OneNote offers more than two dozen tags in the Tags gallery, but if they aren't descriptive enough, you can create tags of your own.

To create a tag, start by clicking More in the Tags gallery. This button is located below the scroll bar. Clicking it opens the gallery. With the gallery open, choose Customize tag on the gallery. Then, in the Customize Tags dialog box, click the New Tag button. You see the New Tag dialog box, in which you can enter a name, choose a symbol, choose a font color, and choose a highlight color for your tag.

Customize a Tag

1. Click the Home tab.

2. Click More on the Tags gallery to open this gallery.

3. Choose Customize Tags.

4. Click the New Tag button to open the New Tag dialog box.

5. In the Display Name text box, enter a name for the tag.

6. Open the Symbol menu and choose a symbol for the tag.

7. Open the Font Color menu and choose a font color for the tag name.

8. Click OK.

9. In the Custom Tags dialog box, click the Move Tag Down button to move the customized tag one position lower in the Tags gallery.

10. Click OK.

Tip

The first eight tags in the Tags gallery are assigned the shortcut keys Ctrl+1 through Ctrl+8. To give a customized tag a keyboard shortcut, move the customized tag to one of the first eight positions in the Tags gallery.

Tip

If you choose a check box symbol for your tag in the New Tag dialog box, you can check off the tag to indicate, for example, when a task is complete or a project is finished. What's more, when you search for tagged items, you can narrow the search to tags that have been checked off.

Modify a Tag

① Click the Home tab.

② Click More in the Tags gallery to open this gallery.

③ Right-click the tag you want to modify and choose Modify This Tag.

④ In the Modify Tag dialog box, change the display name, symbol, font color, and/or the highlight color.

⑤ Click OK.

Caution

OneNote doesn't update existing tags when you modify a tag. If you change the symbol in a tag, the old symbol remains on notes you previously tagged.

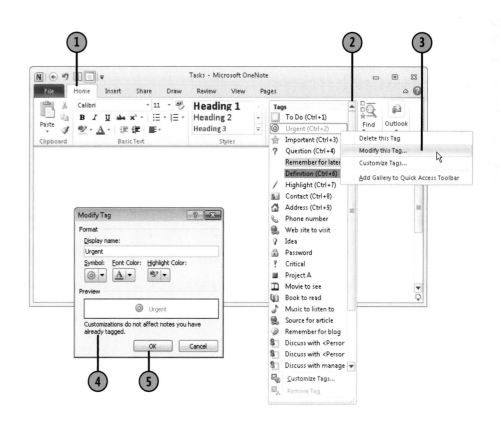

Delete a Tag from the Tags Gallery

① Click the Home tab.

② In the Tags gallery, locate the tag you want to delete.

③ Right-click the tag you want to delete and choose Delete This Tag.

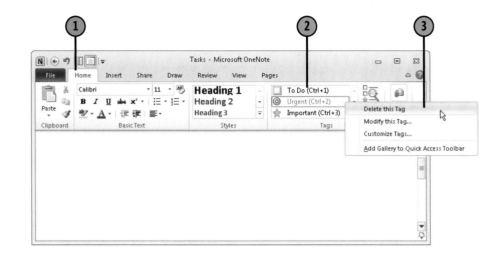

Finding Tagged Notes

OneNote provides the Tags Summary task pane for locating tagged notes. To open the Tags Summary task pane, go to the Home tab and click the Find Tags button. After you conduct a search, you can click an item in the search results and open the page where the tagged note is located.

When you open the task pane, it lists all tagged notes. Use the task pane to narrow the scope of the search and tell OneNote how to arrange, or group, items found in the search.

- Group Tags By: Choose how to list search results in the task pane: under tag names (Tag Name), section names (Section), or page titles (Title), by date (Date), or in alphabetical order by note content (Note Text).

- Show Only Unchecked Items: Select this option when searching for tags with a check box symbol (the To Do tag, for example) to locate only items that have been checked off.

Find Tagged Items

① Click the Home tab.

② Click the Find Tags button to open the Tags Summary task pane.

③ In the Group Tags By menu, choose Section to arrange the search results by section name.

④ In the Search menu, choose This Section.

⑤ Click a tagged item in the search results to go to the page where the item is located.

⑥ Click the Create Summary Page button.

- Search: Choose a scope for the search. The first five options are for searching in groups, sections, and notebooks; the last five are for searching in time periods.

Click the Create Summary Page button in the task pane to create a new page with a copy of all tagged items found in your search. Copying the items to a new page is a convenient way to have a look at all tagged items you found.

Click the Refresh Results button in the Tags Summary task pane when you want to update the results of the search.

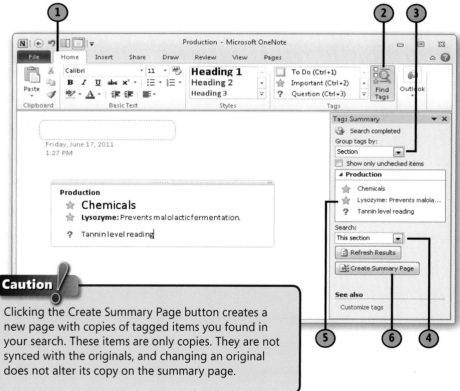

Caution!

Clicking the Create Summary Page button creates a new page with copies of tagged items you found in your search. These items are only copies. They are not synced with the originals, and changing an original does not alter its copy on the summary page.

Color-Coding Notebooks, Sections, and Pages

Color-code notebooks, sections, and pages to make it easier to recognize and find notes. For example, to distinguish notes pertaining to a specific project, make pages where those notes are kept green. To quickly identify a section by color, color-code it with a specific color.

Use these techniques to color-code:

- Page: Select a page, go to the View tab, click the Page Color button, and select a color on the gallery. The page is given a background in the color you selected.

- Section: Right-click the section tab, choose Select Color on the shortcut menu, and select a color on the submenu.

- Notebook: Right-click the notebook's name and choose Properties on the shortcut menu. Then, in the Notebook Properties dialog box, open the Color gallery and select a color. Then click OK. The icon next to the notebook's name appears in the color you selected.

Color-Code a Page and Section

1. Click the View tab.
2. Open the page that needs a new color.
3. Click the Page Color button.
4. Choose a color on the gallery.
5. Right-click a section tab.
6. Choose Section Color.
7. Select a color on the submenu.

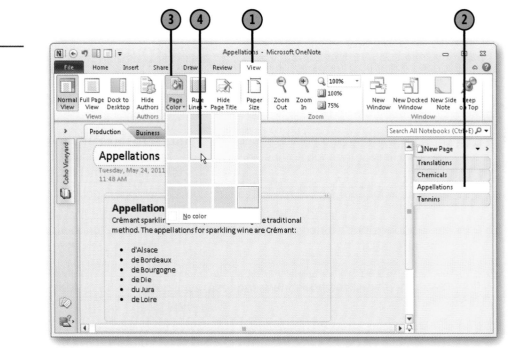

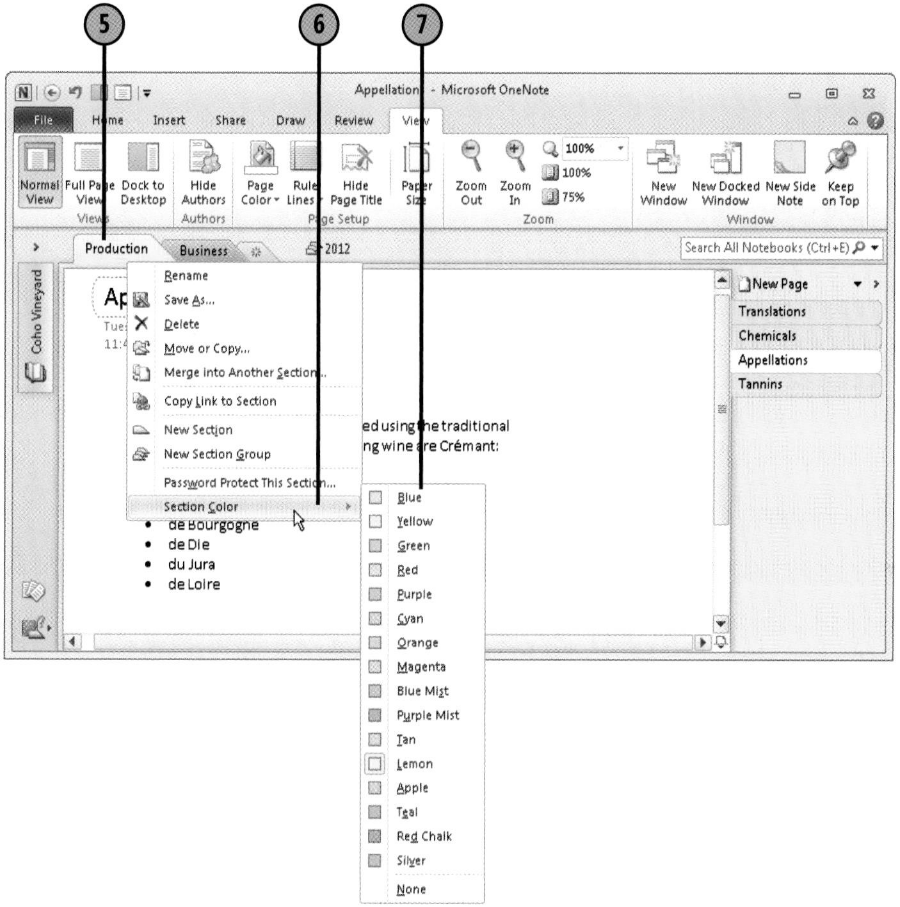
5
6
7
Appellations - Microsoft OneNote
File
Home
Insert
Share
Draw
Review
View
Normal View
Full Page View
Dock to Desktop
Hide Authors
Page Color
Rule Lines
Hide Page Title
Paper Size
Zoom Out
Zoom In
100%
75%
New Window
New Docked Window
New Side Note
Keep on Top
Views
Authors
Page Setup
Zoom
Window
Production
Business
2012
Search All Notebooks (Ctrl+E)
Coho Vineyard
Rename
Save As...
Delete
Move or Copy...
Merge into Another Section...
Copy Link to Section
New Section
New Section Group
Password Protect This Section...
Section Color
Blue
Yellow
Green
Red
Purple
Cyan
Orange
Magenta
Blue Mist
Purple Mist
Tan
Lemon
Apple
Teal
Red Chalk
Silver
None
New Page
Translations
Chemicals
Appellations
Tannins
ed using the traditional
ng wine are Crémant:
de Bourgogne
de Die
du Jura
de Loire

13

Searching for Stray Notes

OneNote provides the Search In box for finding stray notes. This box is located in the upper right of the screen, above the page tabs. To conduct a search, enter a search term in the Search In box.

You can restrict searches to the currently open page, section, section group, or notebook, as well as search all open notebooks.

When searching the currently open page, the search term you entered is highlighted on the page so you can find notes with the search term. When searching sections, section groups, and notebooks, pages where the search term is found are listed. By clicking a page name on the list, you can preview the page where the search term is found; the search term is highlighted on the preview page so you can find it easily.

After your initial search, you can press Alt+O to open the Search Results pane, change the scope of your search, and sort the search results by section name, page title, or date modified.

Initially in a search, OneNote searches the default search scope: the currently open section, section group, or notebook, or all notebooks. You can choose a default search scope for your searches.

Searching a Page

To locate a note on the currently open page, choose the Find on This Page command and enter a search term in the Search In box. This box is located above the page tabs.

To choose the Find on This Page command, press Ctrl+F or open the Change Search Scope menu and choose Find on This Page.

After you enter a search term, instances of the term are highlighted in yellow on the page, and OneNote lists how many matches it found. Use these techniques to find notes containing the search term:

- Scroll the page.
- Click the Next Match button (or press F3) to scroll to the next note with the search term.
- Click the Previous Match button (or press Shift+F3) to scroll to the previous note with the search term.

Press Esc when you finish searching.

Search a Page

1. Open the page you want to search.
2. Press Ctrl+F (or open the Change Search Scope menu and choose Find on This Page).
3. In the Search In box, enter a search term.
4. Scroll in the page to examine notes with the search term.
5. Click the Next Match button (or press F3).
6. Click the Previous Match button (or press Shift+F3).
7. Press Esc to close the Search Results list.

Tip ✓

Search terms are not case-sensitive. You can enter search terms without regard to how you capitalize letters.

Searching a Section, Section Group, or Notebook

To search a section, section group, or notebook, start by opening a page in the section, section group, or notebook. Then enter a search term in the Search In box, and on the Change Search Scope menu, choose This Section, This Section Group, or This Notebook.

OneNote lists pages with notes containing your search term. As well, it lists pages in the Recycle Bin with notes containing your search term. Moreover, the "Recent Picks" section of the search results lists pages with the search term that you recently visited.

By clicking a page name in the search results, you can preview the page. On the preview page, the search term you used in your search is highlighted in notes. To open the page being previewed, click the preview page. When you open a page, OneNote closes the search results list.

Search a section

① Open the Change Search Scope menu and choose This Section.

② In the Search In box, enter a search term.

③ Click a page name in the search results to preview the page.

④ Click the preview page (or press Enter) to open the page and also close the search results list.

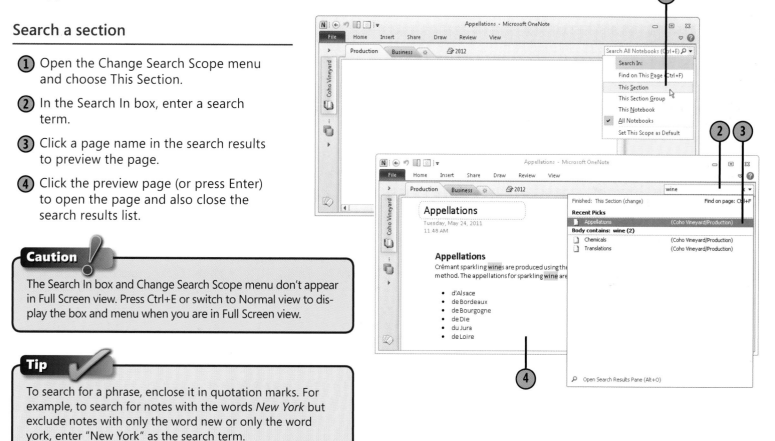

Caution

The Search In box and Change Search Scope menu don't appear in Full Screen view. Press Ctrl+E or switch to Normal view to display the box and menu when you are in Full Screen view.

Tip

To search for a phrase, enclose it in quotation marks. For example, to search for notes with the words *New York* but exclude notes with only the word new or only the word york, enter "New York" as the search term.

Searching All Open Notebooks

To search more than one notebook, the notebooks must be open. Make sure the Navigation bar lists all notebooks you want to search before you start searching more than one notebook.

Click in the Search In box (or press Ctrl+E), enter a search term, and then open the Change Search Scope menu and choose All Notebooks.

In the search results, OneNote lists pages where the search term is found. For each page, it also lists the notebook and section where the page is located. Pages with the search term in the

Recycle Bin and pages with the search term you recently visited are listed as well.

Click a page name to preview it. In the preview page, you can see notes with your search term because the search term is highlighted in yellow.

Click a preview page to open a page. Opening a page closes the search results list.

Search All Open Notebooks

1. Open the notebooks you want to search (make sure their names appear in the Navigation bar).

2. Open the Change Search Scope menu and choose All Notebooks.

3. In the Search In text box, enter a search term.

4. Press the Down Arrow several times to preview several pages with notes containing the search term.

5. Click the preview page (or press Enter) to open the page and also close the search results list.

> **Caution**
>
> OneNote can search only notebooks that are open. If you can't find a note, it could be because the notebook where it is located is closed.

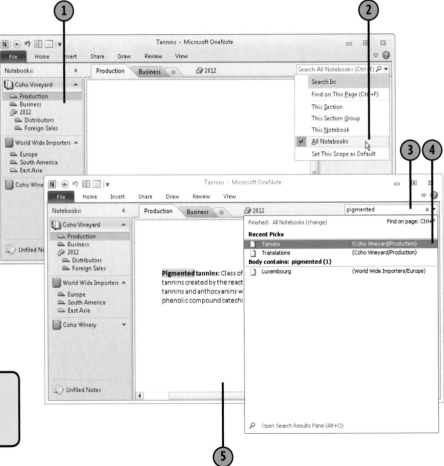

Refining Searches with the Search Results Pane

Sometimes while conducting a search, you need to change the scope. You have to expand or narrow the search to find a note you are looking for.

To refine searches, OneNote offers the Search Results pane. After you initially conduct a search, press Alt+O to open the Search Results pane. It appears on the right side of the screen.

The Search Results pane presents these methods of refining a search:

- On the Change Search Scope menu, choose an option to expand or narrow your search.

- On the Sort by menu, choose an option to sort the search results by section name, page title, or date modified.

Click a page name in the Search Results pane to visit a page. The Search Results pane not only lists the names of pages; it also shows note contents. You can read notes without having to go to a preview page.

Refine a Search with the Search Results Pane

① Press Ctrl+E and enter a search term in the Search In box to conduct a search.

② To open the Search Results pane, press Alt+O (or click the Open Search Results Pane link; it is located at the bottom of the search results list).

(continued on next page)

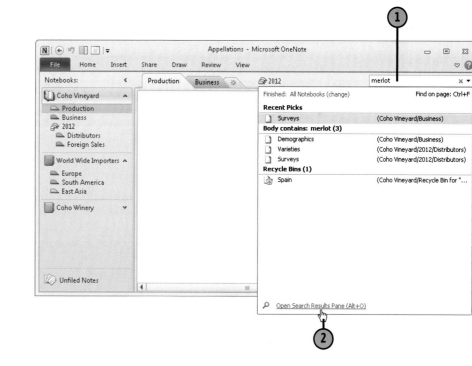

Refine a Search with the Search Results Pane *(continued)*

(3) Open the Change Search Scope menu and choose This Notebook.

(4) Open the Sort By menu and choose Sort by Date Modified.

(5) Click a page name to preview the page.

(6) Click the Close button (or press Esc) to close the Search Results pane.

Choosing the Default Search Scope

When you click in the Search In box (or press Ctrl+E) and enter a search term, OneNote initially searches using the default scope selection: This Section, This Section Group, This Notebook, or All Notebooks. You can tell what the default scope selection is by glancing at the Search box. If it reads "Search All Notebooks (Ctrl+E)," for example, All Notebooks is the default scope, and unless you choose a different search scope, searches begin by finding notes in all open notebooks.

You can change the default search scope so that initial searches find notes in an area of your choice: This Section, This Section Group, This Notebook, or All Notebooks.

To change the default search scope, open the Change Search Scope menu and select the scope option you prefer as the default: This Section, This Section Group, This Notebook, or All Notebooks. Then open the Change Search Scope menu again and choose Set This Scope As Default.

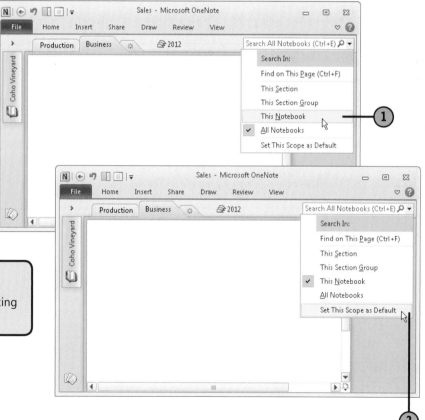

Choose a Default Search Scope

① Open the Change Search Scope menu and choose This Notebook.

② Open the Change Search Scope menu and choose Set This Scope as Default.

Tip ✓

You can always change the search scope in the middle of a search by opening the Change Search Scope menu and making a selection.

14

Housecleaning in OneNote

Sometimes it's necessary to delete a page or section. To do so, right-click the page's name in the pages tab or the section's name in the Navigation bar and choose Delete on the shortcut menu.

Pages and sections that you delete are not really deleted; they are placed in a recycle bin. OneNote maintains one recycle bin for each notebook you create. To recover a page or section, you can open the recycle bin and get it from there.

Notebooks are backed up automatically. You can decide where to keep backup copies of notebooks, how often to back up notebooks, and how many backup copies to keep on hand. Moreover, you can manually back up a notebook whenever you want.

OneNote provides the Open Backups command for examining and copying notes, pages, and sections in backup copies of notebooks.

Deleting a Page

When you don't need a page anymore, delete it. You can delete more than one page at a time. To delete a page, right-click its name in the page tabs and choose Delete.

Delete a Page

1. Display the name of the page that needs deleting on the page tabs.

2. On the page tabs, right-click the name of the page and choose Delete.

3. Ctrl+click page names on the page tabs to select more than one page.

4. Right-click one of the page names you selected and choose Delete.

5. Click the Undo button twice to restore the pages you deleted.

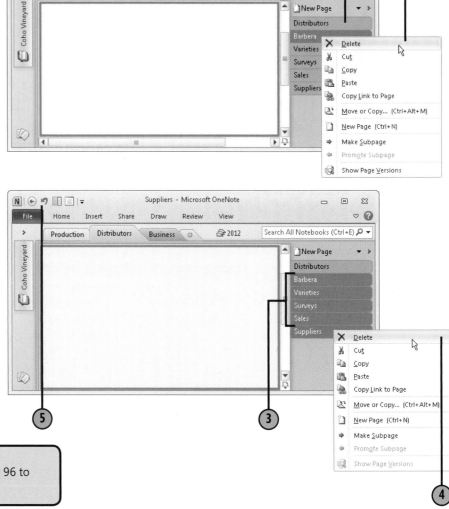

See Also

"Restoring Pages and Sections from the Recycle Bin" on page 156 to learn how to recover a page you deleted.

See Also

"Handling the Navigation Bar and Page Tabs" on page 96 to learn how to display and collapse the page tabs.

Deleting a Section

Delete a section when you no longer need it. To delete a section, right-click its name on the Navigation bar or in the section tabs, and choose Delete on the shortcut menu.

Be careful about deleting sections. You can't restore a section you deleted by clicking the Undo button. The only way to restore a deleted section is to fish it from the recycle bin.

Delete a Section

(1) In the Navigation bar, right-click the name of a section.

(2) Choose Delete on the shortcut menu.

Caution

Unlike when you delete a page, you can't use the Undo button to restore a section you deleted.

See Also

"Restoring Pages and Sections from the Recycle Bin" on page 156 to learn how to recover a section you deleted.

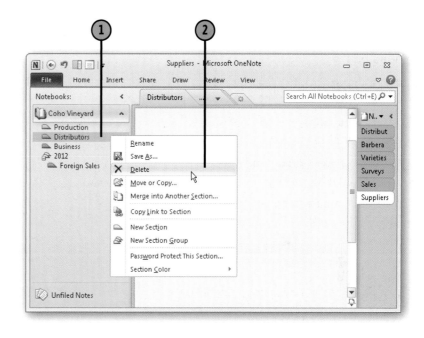

Restoring Pages and Sections from the Recycle Bin

Pages and sections that you delete go to the recycle bin, in which they remain for 60 days. As long as 60 days have not passed since you deleted a page or section, you can restore it. To open the recycle bin, go to the Share tab and click the Notebook Recycle Bin button.

In the recycle bin, deleted pages are stored on the Deleted Pages tab. The names of deleted sections appear in the section tabs.

To restore a page or section from the recycle bin, move the page or section back to your notebook using the standard commands for moving pages and sections (right-click and choose Move or Copy).

Restore a Page from the Recycle Bin

① Click the Share tab.

② Click Notebook Recycle Bin to open the recycle bin.

③ Click the Deleted Pages tab.

④ Right-click a page name on the pages tab and choose Move or Copy (or press Ctrl+Alt+M).

⑤ In the Move or Copy Pages dialog box, select the section where you want to restore the page.

⑥ Click Move.

⑦ Click the Navigate to Parent Section Group button to return to your notebook.

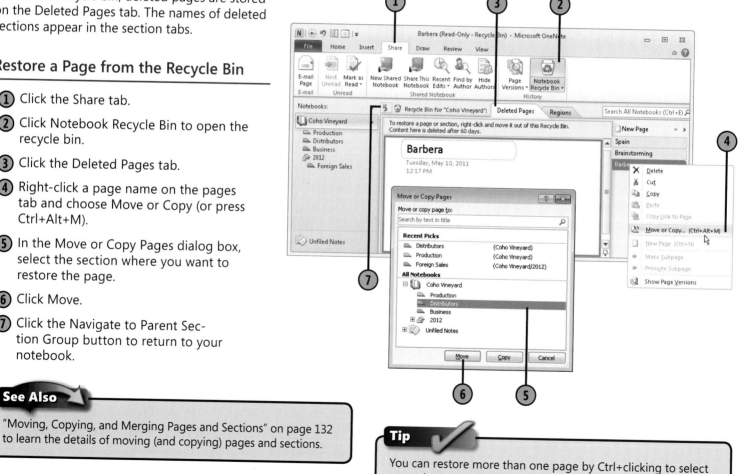

See Also

"Moving, Copying, and Merging Pages and Sections" on page 132 to learn the details of moving (and copying) pages and sections.

Tip

You can restore more than one page by Ctrl+clicking to select more than one page on the pages tab.

Restore a Section from the Recycle Bin

① Click the Share tab.

② Click Notebook Recycle Bin to open the recycle bin.

③ Right-click a section name on the section tabs and choose Move or Copy (or press Ctrl+Alt+M).

④ In the Move or Copy Section dialog box, select a notebook or section to indicate where you want to restore the section.

⑤ Click Move.

⑥ Click the Navigate to Parent Section Group button to return to your notebook.

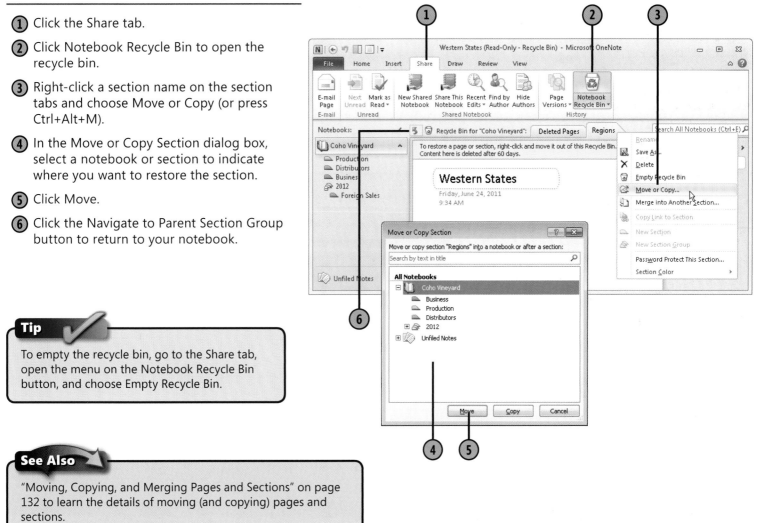

Tip ✓

To empty the recycle bin, go to the Share tab, open the menu on the Notebook Recycle Bin button, and choose Empty Recycle Bin.

See Also

"Moving, Copying, and Merging Pages and Sections" on page 132 to learn the details of moving (and copying) pages and sections.

Backing Up Notebooks Manually

OneNote backs up all notebooks automatically. However, you can back up a notebook at any time in the Save & Backup area of the OneNote Options dialog box. By clicking the Back Up All Notebooks Now button, you can manually back up all notebooks on your computer or network.

Back Up Notebooks Manually

1. Click File.
2. Choose Options.
3. Select Save & Backup
4. Click Back Up All Notebooks Now.
5. Click OK in the Completed Successfully message box.
6. Click OK to close the OneNote Options dialog box.

Tip

Rather than click Back Up All Notebooks Now, click Back Up Changed Files Now to back up only notebooks that have been edited since they were last backed up.

See Also

"Choosing How to Back Up Notebooks" on page 159 to learn how to tell OneNote how often to back up notebooks automatically.

Choosing How to Back Up Notebooks

OneNote backs up all your notebooks automatically. How the backups are made is up to you. You can choose how often notebooks are backed up and how many backup copies to keep.

Choose How to Back Up Notebooks

① Click File.

② Choose Options.

③ Click Save & Backup.

④ Select Automatically Back Up My Notebook at the Following Time Interval.

⑤ In the Automatically Back Up gallery, choose 2 Days.

⑥ In the Number of Backup Copies to Keep menu, choose 2.

⑦ Click OK.

Tip ✓

If you prefer not to keep backup copies of a notebook, go to the Share tab, open the menu on the Notebook Recycle Bin button, and choose Disable History for This Notebook.

Opening a Backup Copy of a Notebook Section

OneNote keeps backup copies of your notebooks. These backup copies of notebooks are maintained in the form of sections. The sections have the file extension .one. For example, the backup copy of a section called "Production" is called "Production.one." To help identify when backup copies were made, OneNote lists the date they were made after the backup name.

To view the backup copy of a section, click File, choose Info, and click the Open Backups button. Then, in the Open Backup dialog box, open the folder with the name of your notebook, select the backup section you want to open, and click the Open button (in the Open Backup dialog box, sections in section groups are stored in a subfolder named after the section group).

After you open a backup copy of a section, OneNote places a tab on the Navigation bar called Open Sections. With this tab, you can switch back and forth between backup sections you opened and your OneNote notebook.

You can copy notes, pages, and the section itself from the backup copy into a notebook.

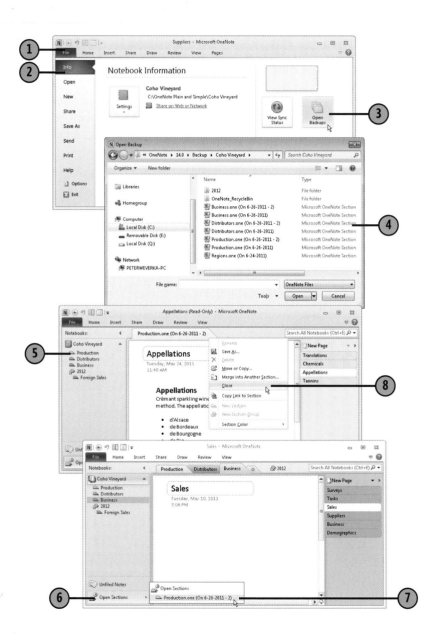

Open a Backup Copy of a Notebook Section

1 Click File.

2 Click Info.

3 Click Open Backups.

4 In the Open Backup dialog box, locate the backup copy of the section you want to open, select it, and click the Open button.

5 Select a section in your notebook to return to your notebook.

6 In your notebook, click Open Sections on the Navigation bar.

7 Choose the name of the backup notebook section to return to it.

8 On the section tabs, right-click the backup section and choose Close to close the backup section.

Tip

You can copy pages and sections from a backup notebook section by using standard copying techniques (right-click; choose a page or section; choose Move or Copy; and in the Move and Copy dialog box, select a section and click Copy).

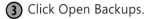

Try This!

To find out where the Backup folder is located, click File, choose Options, and go to the Save & Backup area of the OneNote Options dialog box. Then, under Save, look for the path to the Backup folder. You can double-click this path in the OneNote Options dialog box to open the Backup folder in Computer.

15

Conducting Research in OneNote 2010

The Research task pane offers dictionaries, thesauruses, Internet searching, and translation services. In addition, you can do financial research. And best of all, you can conduct your research inside Microsoft OneNote 2010 without having to open a web browser or other application.

You can do the following kinds of research with the Research task pane:

- Get a word definition.

- Get language use explanations with the English Assistance option (this option is designed to help people whose native language is not English).

- Find synonyms for a word in a thesaurus.

- Translate a word, phrase, or passage from one language to another. Besides translating in the Research task pane, you can use the Mini Translator.

- Get financial information.

The Research task pane is available in all Microsoft Office 2010 applications as well as OneNote. You can take advantage of this nifty tool wherever you go in Office 2010.

Handling the Research Task Pane

The Research task pane is convenient for conducting all kinds of research, but it has one drawback: it can get in the way. You can, however, open and close the Research task pane very easily. And you can move, resize, and dock it as well with a few simple techniques.

Open, Resize, Move, Dock, and Close the Research Task Pane

1 Click the Review tab.

2 Click Research to make the Research task pane appear.

3 Hover the pointer over the left boundary of the Research task pane, and when the pointer shows a two-headed arrow, click and drag to resize the task pane.

4 Hover the pointer over the Research taskbar (or open the Task Pane Options menu and choose Move) so that the pointer shows a four-headed arrow.

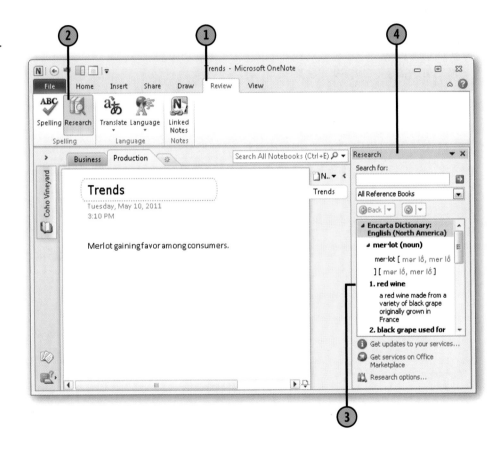

5 Click and drag the Research taskbar to move the Research task pane into the middle of the screen.

6 Hover the pointer over the lower-right corner of the Research task pane (or open the Task Pane Options menu and choose Size), and with the pointer showing a two-headed arrow, drag the lower-right corner of the Research task pane to change its size.

7 Double-click the Research taskbar to dock the Research task pane on the right side of the OneNote screen.

(continued on next page)

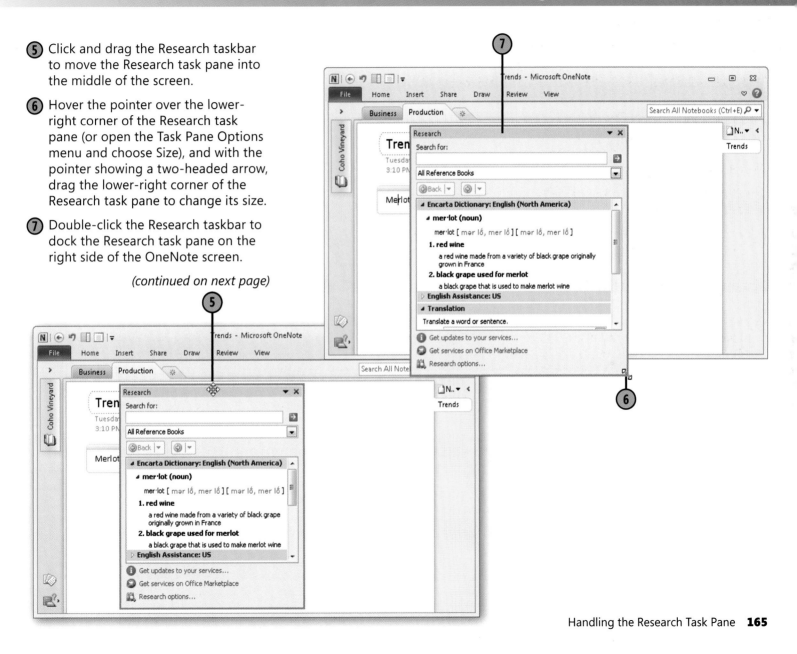

⑧ Click the Close button on the Research taskbar to close the Research task pane.

You can close the Research task pane with any of these techniques:

- Click the Research button on the Review tab (this button is a toggle; clicking it closes as well as opens the Research task pane).
- Click the Close button on the Research taskbar.
- Open the Task Pane Options menu on the Research taskbar and choose Close.

A fast way to open the Research task pane and conduct research is to right-click a word in a note and choose Look Up.

Researching a Topic

Use the Research task pane when you need more information for a note. The Research task pane offers dictionaries, thesauruses, and Internet searching. When you conduct an Internet search, you can click a hyperlink in the Research task pane to open a website in your browser.

Speaking of web browsers, the Research task pane, like a browser, offers Back and Forward buttons (and Back and Forward galleries) so you can retrace or revisit search results.

Research a Topic

1. Click the Review tab.

2. Click Research to display the Research task pane.

3. In the Search For text box, enter a term or terms to describe the topic you want information about.

4. Open the Search For gallery and choose a reference book (or All Reference Books), a research site (or All Research Sites), or a Business and Financial site (or All Business and Financial Sites).

(continued on next page)

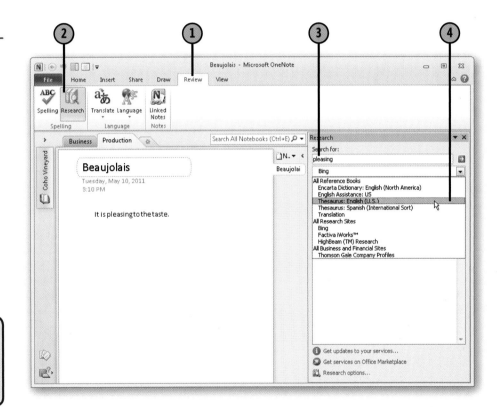

Tip

Rather than enter a search term, you can right-click a word in a note and choose Look Up to quickly open the Research task pane and conduct a search.

Research a Topic *(continued)*

⑤ Scroll through the Research task pane to examine the results of your search.

⑥ Select a search result to turn the search in a different direction.

⑦ Click Back to return to your previous search results.

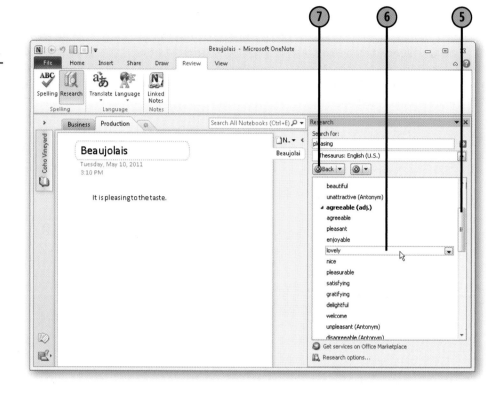

See Also

"Customizing the Research Task Pane" on page 169 to learn how to decide which options appear in the Search For gallery.

Customizing the Research Task Pane

To conduct a search in the Research task pane, you open the Search For gallery and choose a reference book, research site, or business and financial site. Which options appear on the gallery is up to you. Office 2010 offers many different options for the Search For gallery.

To make for faster and better researching, you can confine the options on the Search For gallery to options you like the best or use the most. You can also designate one choice as your favorite. The favorite research option is the one that is used when you right-click a word in a note and choose Look Up.

Customize the Research Task Pane

1️⃣ Click the Review tab.

2️⃣ Click Research to display the Research task pane.

3️⃣ Click Research Options (this link is located at the bottom of the Research task pane).

4️⃣ In the Research Options dialog box, select the Services options you want for the Search For gallery in the Research task pane.

5️⃣ Select the option that you want to use by default when you conduct research (this option is used when you right-click a word in a note and choose Look Up).

6️⃣ Click the Favorite button.

7️⃣ Click OK.

Try This!

Select a Services option in the Research Options dialog box and click the Properties button. A dialog box appears and describes in detail what the option is.

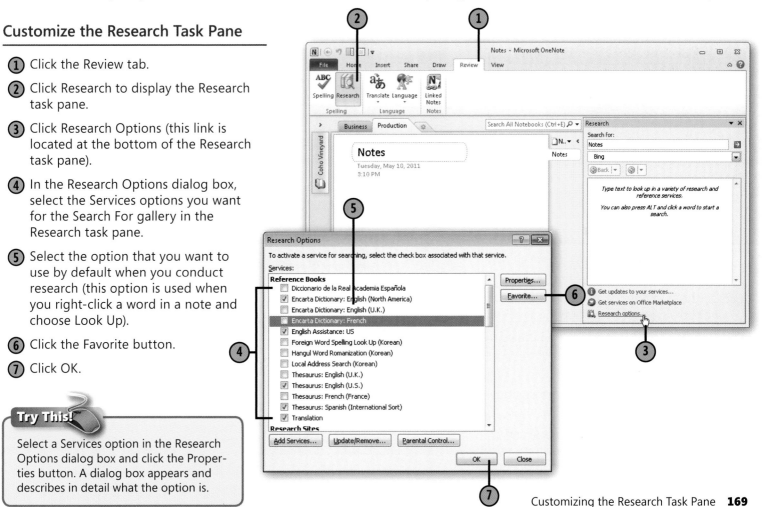

Translating Text

To translate text, OneNote 2010 offers translation services in the Research task pane as well as a little device called the Mini Translator. To translate text with the Mini Translator, all you have to do is select the text, hover the pointer over the text, and read the translation in the Microsoft Translator toolbar.

However, you have to do some setup work before you can use the Mini Translator.

You can translate text not just from English to a foreign language but also from one foreign language to another.

Translate a Word, Phrase, or Passage with the Research Task Pane

1. Drag to select the word, phrase, or passage you want to translate (if you want to translate a single word, you need only to click it).

2. Click the Review tab.

3. Click Translate.

4. Choose Translate Selected Text on the button's gallery.

5. On the From menu in the Research task pane, choose the language in which the text you selected is written.

6. On the To menu, choose the language to which you want to translate the text.

7. Click the Start Searching button (this green button is located to the right of the Search For text box).

8. Open the Insert menu and choose Copy to copy the translation to the Clipboard.

9. Right-click on the OneNote page and choose a Paste option on the shortcut menu to paste the translation into a note.

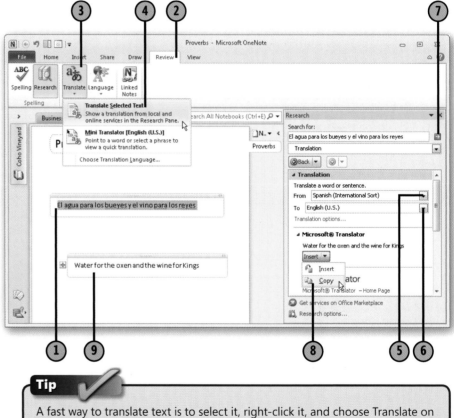

Tip

A fast way to translate text is to select it, right-click it, and choose Translate on the shortcut menu. OneNote translates the text using the previous From and To options you selected. Choose different From and To options if necessary and then click the Start Searching button to complete the translation.

Get Ready to Use the Mini Translator

① Click the Review tab.

② Click Translate.

③ Choose the Choose Translation Language option on the button's gallery.

④ In the Translation Language Options dialog box, choose the language to which you will translate text when using the Mini Translator.

⑤ Click OK.

⑥ Click Translate again.

⑦ Choose Mini Translator on the button's gallery (if necessary because the option isn't selected yet).

Try This!

Click the Translation Options link in the Research task pane. Doing so opens the Translation Options dialog box, in which you can see all the available language pairs (the To and From translation options). If the To and From language pair you need isn't in the Research task pane, select it in this dialog box so you can translate text to and from the languages of your choice.

Caution

To use the Mini Translator, the Mini Translator option must be selected (you see this option when you click Translate on the Review tab). This button is a toggle. You can tell when it is selected because it is highlighted.

Use the Mini Translator

① Select the text you want to translate.

② Hover the pointer over the text, and when you see the Microsoft Translator toolbar, move the pointer onto the toolbar so you can read the translation.

③ Click Copy.

④ Right-click on the OneNote page and choose a Paste option on the shortcut menu to paste the translation into a note.

Try This!

Click Play in the Microsoft Translator toolbar to hear a translation of the text.

Proverbs - Microsoft OneNote

File   Home   Insert   Share   Draw   Review   View

Business   Production

Search All Notebooks (Ctrl+E)

Coho Vineyard

N..

Proverbs

Translatio

Proverbs

Tuesday, May 10, 2011
3:10 PM

Water for the oxen and the wine for kings.

Microsoft® Translator
Agua para los bueyes y el vino para los Reyes.

Microsoft® Translator
Agua para los bueyes y el vino para los Reyes.

16

Distributing Your Notes

To distribute notes, you can print them, email them, and save them in many common file formats, including PDF, XPS, and MHT.

Moreover, Microsoft OneNote 2010 offers a special file format—the OneNote Package format—for transferring a notebook from one computer to another. Rather than meticulously copying all the section files that make up a notebook, you can save your notebook as a OneNote 2010 Package file and then simply open this file on the other computer.

Printing a Section

Using the standard Print command, you can print all or some of the pages in a section. To print, OneNote presents the same Print dialog box as the other Microsoft Office 2010 applications.

Print a Section

1. Open the section you want to print.
2. Click File.
3. Choose Print.
4. Click Print.
5. Choose settings in the Print dialog box (enter individual pages or page ranges in the Pages box to print some, not all, pages in a section).
6. Click the Print button.

Tip ✓

Follow these steps to see what a section will look like before you print it (and print the section as well):

1. Click the File tab
2. Click Print.
3. Click Print Preview.
4. In the Print Preview and Settings screen, under Print Range, choose Current Section.
5. Click the Previous and Next Page buttons to preview all the pages in the section.
6. Change print settings if you want.
7. Click the Print button.

Tip ✓

You can press Ctrl+P to open the Print dialog box without clicking the File tab and choosing Print.

Emailing a Page

When you give a command to send a page by email, a Microsoft Outlook 2010 message window opens automatically so you can address the email message. As well, you can write a message in the window to accompany the OneNote page you send.

OneNote offers three methods to send all the notes on a page by email:

- E-mail page: Send the notes on the page as text inside the email message. Use this method to send a page to someone who doesn't have OneNote.

- E-mail as attachment: Send the page as two file attachments. With this technique, a section (.one) file and single file web page (.mht) file are sent. The recipient can open the .one file in OneNote and the .mht file in Internet Explorer. Use this method to send a page to someone who has OneNote.

- E-mail page as PDF: Send the page itself as a .pdf file. These files can be read in Adobe Reader. Use this method to send the page to someone who doesn't have OneNote but wants to preserve the notes in a file and read them using Adobe Reader.

Email a Page

1. Open the page you want to send by email.

2. Click File.

3. Choose Send.

4. Click E-Mail Page as Attachment.

5. Enter an address in the message window.

6. Enter a message to accompany the attached files.

7. Click Send.

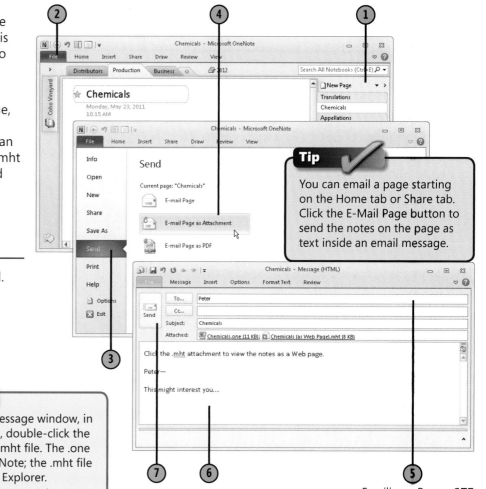

Tip

You can email a page starting on the Home tab or Share tab. Click the E-Mail Page button to send the notes on the page as text inside an email message.

Try This!

In the Outlook message window, in the Attached box, double-click the .one file and the .mht file. The .one file opens in OneNote; the .mht file opens in Internet Explorer.

Saving Pages, Sections, and Notebooks in Alternative File Formats

Save OneNote material in an alternative file format so that others who don't have OneNote can read the material. OneNote offers a host of different ways to save pages, sections, and notebooks in alternative file formats.

To save in a different format, click the File tab and choose Save As to open the Save As window. From there, choose whether you want to save a page, section, or your notebook; choose a file format; and click the Save As button.

OneNote offers these Save As options:

Option	Saves	As
OneNote 2010 section (*.one)	A page or section	A OneNote 2010 section file.
OneNote 2007 section (*.one)	A page or section	A OneNote 2007 section file. Use this option for backward compatibility to give a page or section to someone running OneNote 2007.
Word document (*.docx)	A page or section	A Word document. The document can be read and edited in Word 2010 and 2007.
Word 97-2003 document (*.doc)	A page or section	A Word 97-2003 document. The document can be read and edited in Word 2003 and prior versions of Word.
PDF (*.pdf)	A page, section, or notebook	A Portable Document Format file. The file can be read in Adobe Reader.
XPS (*.xps)	A page, section, or notebook	An XML Paper Specification file. The file can be read using XPS Viewer (available in Windows Vista and Windows 7).
Single File Web Page (*.mht)	A page or section	A Single File Web Page Format file. The file can be viewed in Internet Explorer.
OneNote Package (*.onepkg)	A notebook	A OneNote Package Format file. Choose this option to transfer a notebook from one computer to another.

Save a Page, Section, or Notebook to an Alternative File Format

1. To save a page or section in a different format, open the page or section.

2. Click File.

3. Choose Save As.

4. Choose Section.

5. Choose PDF (*.pdf).

6. Click the Save As button.

7. In the Save As dialog box, choose a folder for storing the section and click the Save button.

See Also

"Transferring a Notebook to Another Computer" on page 178 to learn how to save a notebook as a OneNote Package file on your computer and open this file on a second computer.

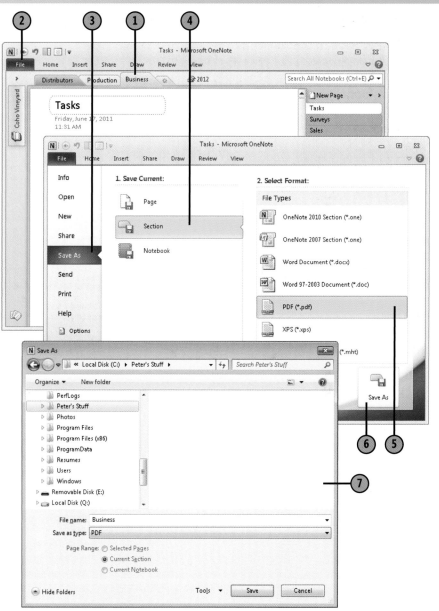

Transferring a Notebook to Another Computer

OneNote provides a special file format for transferring notebooks between computers. The file format is called OneNote Package (*.onepkg). To transfer a notebook to another computer, first save it as a OneNote Package file. Then move or copy this file to the second computer and open it. When you open the file, OneNote converts the OneNote Package file to a OneNote 2010 notebook.

Transfer a Notebook to Another Computer

1. Open the notebook.
2. Click File.
3. Choose Save As.
4. Choose Notebook.
5. Choose OneNote Package (*.onepkg).
6. Click Save As.
7. In the Save As dialog box, choose a folder or disk for storing the OneNote package file, and click Save.
8. Copy or move the file to the other computer.

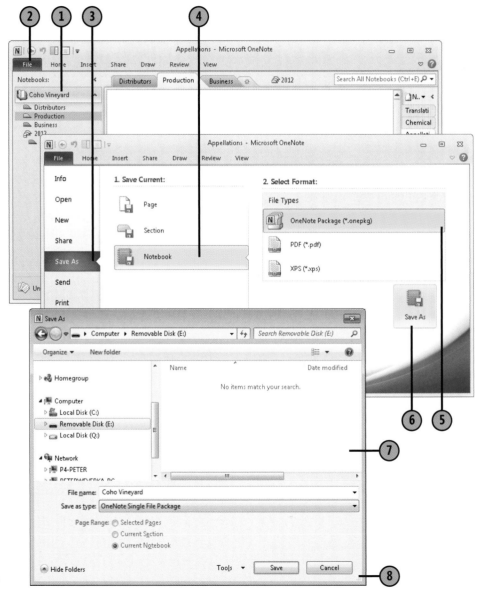

(9) In OneNote on the other computer, click File.

(10) Choose Open.

(11) Click Open Notebook.

(12) In the Open Notebook dialog box, open the File Type menu and choose OneNote Single File Package.

(13) Select the notebook you saved as a OneNote package file.

(14) Click the Open button.

17

Using OneNote with Other Office 2010 Applications

OneNote works hand in glove with two other Microsoft Office 2010 applications: Microsoft Word 2010 and Microsoft Outlook 2010.

In the case of Word, you can open a OneNote page in Word 2010. All formats except styles transfer to the Word page. After you edit the page in Word, you can save it as a Word document.

In the case of Outlook 2010, you can create an Outlook task in OneNote without having to open Outlook, and you can get information about a meeting directly from Outlook as well.

On the idea that you want to take notes about the email messages, meetings, contacts, and tasks that you track in Outlook, Outlook offers the OneNote button for copying data from Outlook to OneNote. After you select an email message, meeting, contact, or task in Outlook, you can click the OneNote button to copy the item to OneNote. Moreover, when you copy a meeting, contact, or task, OneNote includes a link that you can click to return to Outlook when you need to.

Opening a Page in Word

OneNote offers a command for opening a page in Word. Use this command to take advantage of the numerous editing tools that are available in Word. After you open the page in Word, you can edit and save it as a Word document.

Open a Page in Word

1. Go to the page you want to open in Word and make sure the cursor is located on that page.

2. Click File.

3. Choose Send.

4. Click Send to Word.

See Also

"Creating Links to Web Pages and Files" on page 87 to learn how to put a file link in a note so you can click the link and open the file.

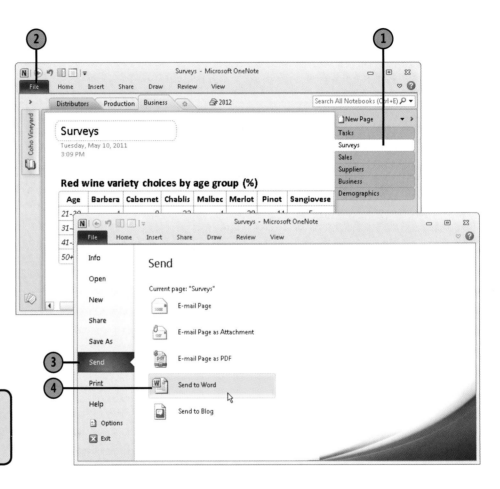

Creating an Outlook Task in OneNote

Outlook offers the Tasks window for recording and tracking tasks. When you create a task, you record its start date and due date. You can glance at the Tasks window in Outlook to see what needs doing and when it's due, and plan your time accordingly.

OneNote gives you the opportunity to create a task without opening Outlook. The tasks are recorded both on a OneNote page and in Outlook. You can switch between the task in OneNote and the task in Outlook, and in this way you can keep notes about tasks.

To create an Outlook task in OneNote, start by writing a note that describes the task. The description doubles as a note and task name. For example, a note with the text "Gather data for emerging market analysis" is recorded in the Outlook Tasks window as this task: "Gather data for emerging market analysis."

After you write the note, click in the note and use one of these techniques to create an Outlook task:

- On the Home tab, click the Outlook Tasks button and choose a due date for the task on the gallery.

- Right-click, choose Outlook Tasks on the shortcut menu and choose a due date for the task on the submenu.

In OneNote, tasks are marked with the task icon, a red flag. Without leaving OneNote, you can manage tasks with these techniques:

- Mark a task as complete: Right-click the task icon and choose Mark Complete, or click the Outlook Tasks button and choose Mark Complete. Tasks that are marked as complete show the check mark icon, not the red flag.

- Delete a task: Right-click the task icon and choose Delete Outlook Task, click the Outlook Tasks button and choose Delete Outlook Task, or press Ctrl+Shift+0.

- Change the due date: Right-click the task icon and choose a different due date, click the Outlook Tasks button and choose a different due date, or press a shortcut key (Ctrl+Shift+1, 2, 3, 4, 5, or K).

- Open the task in an Outlook Task window: Right-click the task icon and choose Open Task in Outlook, or click the Outlook Tasks button and choose Open Task in Outlook. A Task window opens (this window is used for addressing individual tasks). From here, you can forward the task, assign it to someone, and make the task a recurring task, among other things.

In Outlook, tasks you create in OneNote are linked to the OneNote page in which they were created. In an Outlook Task window, you can double-click the link to OneNote to open the OneNote page where the task was created. In this way, you can read notes about tasks and stay on top of your work.

Create an Outlook Task in OneNote

① Click the note you want to create as a task.

② Click the Home tab.

③ Click Outlook Tasks.

④ Choose This Week.

⑤ Right-click the task icon and choose Today to change the due date.

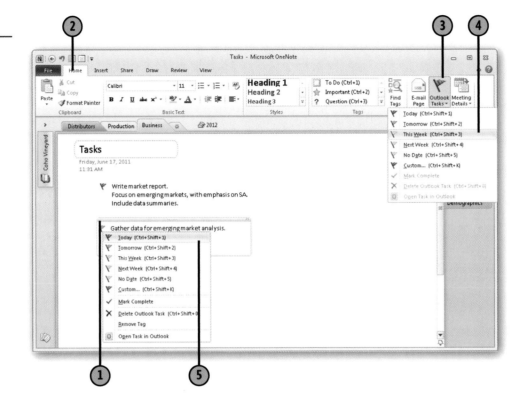

(6) Open Outlook.

(7) Open the Tasks folder.

(8) Double-click the task you created to open it in a Task window.

(9) Double-click the Link to Task in One-Note link to open the OneNote page where the task was created.

Entering Meeting Details from Outlook in a Note

Using the Calendar, you can schedule meetings in Outlook. When you schedule a meeting, you enter its name; its date and time; and, if you want, a description.

OneNote offers the Meeting Details command to place meeting information from Outlook in a note. The information appears in a table. Below the table, you can write your thoughts about the meeting and in so doing prepare yourself for it.

To get details about a meeting, go to the Home tab and click the Meeting Details button. The gallery presents com-

mands for entering information about meetings scheduled for today, past days, and future days:

- Today: Click the name of the meeting on the gallery.

- Past and future days: Select Choose a Meeting from Another Day. The Insert Outlook Meeting Details dialog box opens. Using the Previous Day button, Next Day button, and the Calendar, locate a meeting. Then select it and click the Insert Details button.

Enter Meeting Details from Outlook in a Note

1. Click the Home tab.
2. Click Meeting Details.
3. Select Choose a Meeting from Another Day.
4. Click Calendar and select a day with a scheduled meeting.
5. Select a meeting.
6. Click Insert Details.

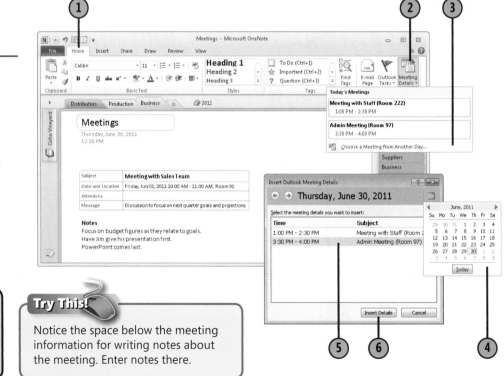

See Also

"Entering Outlook Information (Email, Meeting, Contact, Task) on a Page" on page 187 to learn how to send meeting details to OneNote by starting in Outlook.

Try This!

Notice the space below the meeting information for writing notes about the meeting. Enter notes there.

Entering Outlook Information (Email, Meeting, Contact, Task) on a Page

In Outlook, you can click the OneNote button to copy information from Outlook to OneNote. You can copy email messages, meetings, contacts, and tasks. Copy this information from Outlook if you need to keep notes about email messages, meetings, contacts, or tasks. In the case of meetings, contacts, and tasks, OneNote not only copies the information but it also provides a link that you can click to open the meeting, contact, or task in Outlook.

By default, after you click the OneNote button to copy information to OneNote, the Select Location in OneNote dialog box appears so you can choose where to copy the information.

You can, however, choose options in the OneNote Options dialog box (in the Send to OneNote area) to determine how information is sent from Outlook to OneNote. The options are as follows:

- Always Ask Where to Send: The information is sent to a section of your choice. In the Select Location in OneNote dialog box, choose a section and click OK. (This is the default choice.)

- To Current Page: The information is sent to the currently open page in OneNote.

- To New Page in Current Section: The information is sent to a new page in the currently open section in OneNote.

- Set Default Location: The information is sent to a default section. In the Select Location in OneNote dialog box, choose the section you want as the default and click OK.

This table describes where the OneNote button is located in Outlook and what information is passed to OneNote when you click this button:

Outlook Folder	Button Location	Copies to OneNote
Mail	Mail window (Home tab), Message window	The text of an email, as well as its subject, sender, recipients, and sent date. OneNote creates a new page for the email.
Calendar	Calendar window (Calendar Tools Appointment tab), Appointment window	The meeting name, its date and location, attendees' names, and a link for opening the meeting in Outlook. OneNote creates a new page for the meeting.
Contacts	Contacts window (Home tab), Contact window (Contact tab)	The contact's name and all other information recorded about her or him, as well as a link for opening the contact in Outlook. OneNote creates a new page for the contact.
Tasks	Tasks window (Home tab), Task window (Task tab)	The task's name and a link for opening the task in OneNote. OneNote creates a new page for the task.

Enter Outlook Information on a Page

(1) Open Outlook.

(2) Open the Contacts folder.

(3) Select a contact.

(4) Click the OneNote button.

(5) Select a section.

(6) Click OK.

(7) In OneNote, click the link to view the contact in Outlook.

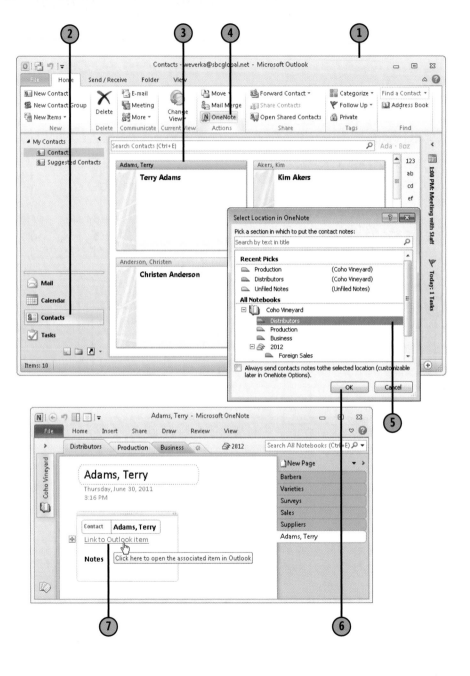

Choose How Outlook Sends Information to OneNote

① Click File.

② Choose Options.

③ Select Send to OneNote.

④ Under Outlook Items, for email messages, meetings, contacts, and tasks, choose how you want to send information to OneNote.

⑤ Click OK.

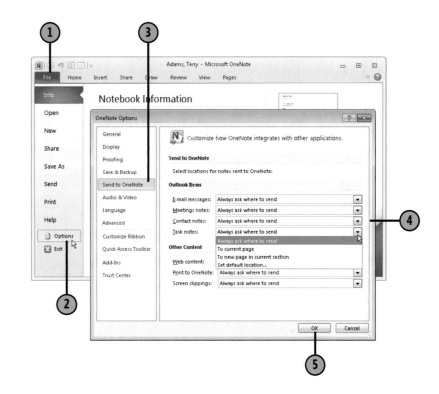

18

Sharing Notebooks with Others

Microsoft OneNote 2010 offers the Share tab to help you collaborate with others on a shared notebook. On the tab are commands for sharing notebooks, finding out who wrote different notes, marking pages with notes you haven't read yet, marking pages that you have read, and finding notes written in your absence.

Sharing notebooks is a great way to pool resources and share information with colleagues, co-workers, or fellow students.

Sharing a Notebook

You can share notebooks on a network, in a folder at Windows Live, or on a Microsoft SharePoint website:

- If your computer is connected to a network, you can share OneNote 2010 notebooks on a network folder.

- Windows Live is an online service from Microsoft for emailing, storing files, and sharing files. Signing up with Windows Live costs nothing. You can share notebooks with other Windows Live users by placing notebooks in a SkyDrive folder on Windows Live. For more information, see Section 20.

- Microsoft SharePoint is a software product designed to help people share files. Users can share OneNote notebooks on a SharePoint website. For information about SharePoint, visit http://sharepoint.microsoft.com.

To create a new notebook and share it with others, go to the Share tab and click the New Shared Notebook button (or click the File button and choose New). In the New Network window, choose Web or Network, enter a name for your notebook, designate a web location or network location, and click the Create Notebook button.

To share a notebook you already created, go to the Share tab and click the Share This Notebook button. In the Share Notebook window, choose Web or Network, designate a web location or network location, and click the Share Notebook button.

Share a Notebook

(1) Click the Share tab.

(2) Click New Shared Notebook (or Share This Notebook to share a notebook you already created).

(3) Choose Web to share the notebook on Windows Live or Network to share it on a network or SharePoint website.

(4) Enter a name for your notebook.

(5) Choose a shared folder on Windows Live or a network location.

(6) Click Create Notebook.

See Also

Section 20, "Using OneNote Web App," on page 215 to learn how to share and collaborate with others on Windows Live using OneNote Web App.

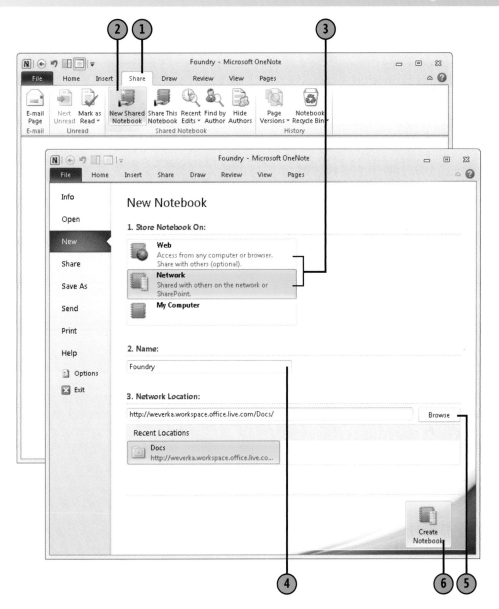

Finding Unread Notes

When you open a notebook that you share with others, notes written by others since the previous time you opened the notebook are highlighted. What's more, in the page tabs, the names of pages with unread notes appear in bold letters.

To open the next page in a notebook with notes you haven't read, go to the Share tab and click the Next Unread button.

On the Share tab, use these techniques to indicate that you've read notes entered by others since the previous time you opened a notebook:

- Click the Mark As Read button (or press Ctrl+Q) to show that you have read new notes on a page. After you click this button, new notes on the page are no longer highlighted; in the page tabs, the page's name is no longer shown in bold letters.

- Click the Mark As Read button and choose Mark Notebook As Read to show you've read all new notes in a notebook. All new notes are no longer highlighted; no names in the page tabs are shown in bold.

If you change your mind about marking the notes on a page as read, click the Mark As Read button and choose Mark As Unread (or press Ctrl+Q).

Find Unread Notes (and Mark Them as Read)

(1) Click the Share tab.

(2) Hover the pointer over an author's initials, and note the author's name and note modification date in the ScreenTip.

(3) Click Next Unread to go to the next page with unread notes.

(4) Click the Mark As Read button to show you read the notes on this page.

(5) Open the gallery on the Mark As Read button and choose Mark Notebook As Read.

> **Tip**
>
> If unread notes are not highlighted, and the names of pages with unread notes are not bold in the page tabs, click the Mark As Read button and choose Show Unread Changes in This Notebook.

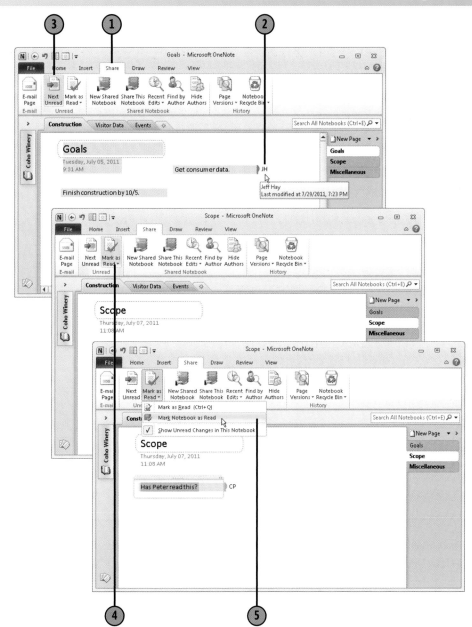

Finding Notes by Specific Authors

Notes are marked with their authors' initials. By moving the pointer over these initials, you can see, in a ScreenTip, the author's name and when he or she wrote the note. (If authors' initials don't appear, click the Hide Authors button on the Share tab.)

To find notes by a specific author, go to the Share tab and click the Find by Author button. The Search Results task pane lists the names of authors who have contributed to the notebook. To read notes by a specific author, click his or her name in the list. Then, under the author's name, click the name of a page to open the page and read the author's notes.

Find Notes by a Specific Author

① Click the Share tab.

② Click Find by Author.

③ Click an author's name.

④ Click a page's name.

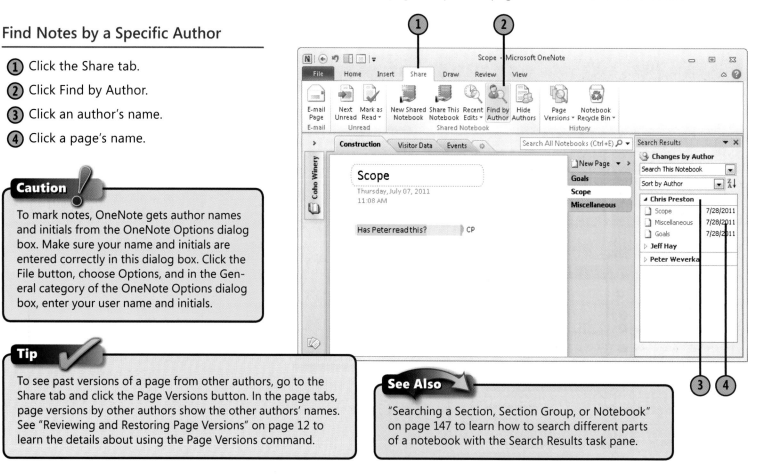

Caution!

To mark notes, OneNote gets author names and initials from the OneNote Options dialog box. Make sure your name and initials are entered correctly in this dialog box. Click the File button, choose Options, and in the General category of the OneNote Options dialog box, enter your user name and initials.

Tip

To see past versions of a page from other authors, go to the Share tab and click the Page Versions button. In the page tabs, page versions by other authors show the other authors' names. See "Reviewing and Restoring Page Versions" on page 12 to learn the details about using the Page Versions command.

See Also

"Searching a Section, Section Group, or Notebook" on page 147 to learn how to search different parts of a notebook with the Search Results task pane.

Finding Recently Edited Notes

Another way to search for notes you haven't read is to show only notes in a specific timeframe. For example, you can tell OneNote to show only notes written or edited in the past week. In this way, you can focus on notes that matter to you.

To display only notes in a certain timeframe, go to the Share tab and click the Recent Edits button. Then, on the menu, choose a timeframe. The Search Results task pane lists pages with notes that were written or edited in the timeframe you chose. Select the name of a page to view its notes.

Find Recently Edited Notes

① Click the Share tab.

② Click Recent Edits.

③ Choose a timeframe.

④ Select a page.

See Also

"Searching a Section, Section Group, or Notebook" on page 147 to learn how to search different parts of a notebook with the Search Results task pane.

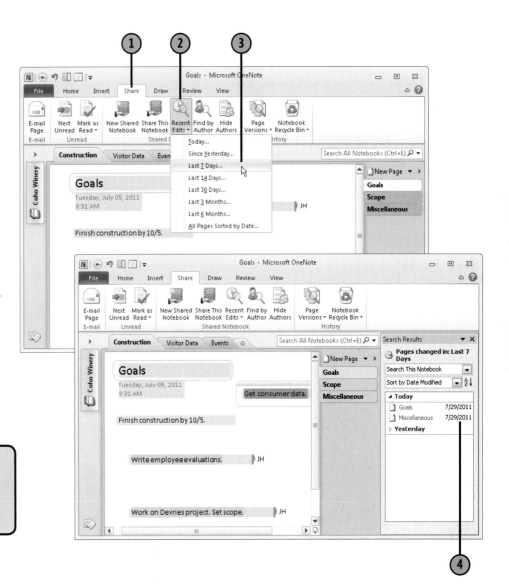

19

Customizing OneNote 2010

Except by pressing keyboard shortcuts, you give commands in OneNote by using the ribbon and the Quick Access toolbar. To make using OneNote easier, you can customize the ribbon and Quick Access toolbar.

You can place the commands you use most often and the commands you find most useful on the ribbon and Quick Access toolbar. You can also remove commands; rearrange commands; and in the case of the ribbon, create your own tabs and command groups on tabs.

OneNote also allows you to place the Quick Access toolbar below the ribbon rather than above it.

If you discover after you customize the Quick Access toolbar or ribbon that you want the original back, you can get it back. OneNote offers Reset commands for restoring the Quick Access toolbar and ribbon to their default settings.

Customizing the Quick Access Toolbar

For your convenience, the Quick Access toolbar appears in the upper-left corner of the screen no matter where you go in OneNote. This toolbar offers a handful of useful buttons you can click: Back, Undo, Dock to Desktop, and Full Page View. Because these commands are on the Quick Access toolbar, they are always available.

OneNote offers the opportunity to add more buttons to and remove buttons from the Quick Access toolbar. You can also change the order of buttons and move the Quick Access toolbar below the ribbon.

Use these techniques to customize the Quick Access toolbar:

- Add buttons: OneNote offers these methods of adding buttons:

  - Right-click a button on any tab and choose Add to Quick Access toolbar.

  - Click the Customize Quick Access Toolbar button (it's located to the right of the toolbar) and choose a button on the gallery.

  - Open the Customize the Quick Access Toolbar window, choose a command, and click the Add button. To open the Customize the Quick Access Toolbar window, right-click the Quick Access toolbar and choose Customize Quick Access Toolbar.

- Remove buttons: OneNote offers these methods of removing buttons from the Quick Access toolbar:

- Right-click a button and choose Remove from Quick Access toolbar.

- Click the Customize Quick Access Toolbar button (located to the right of the toolbar) and clear a button on the gallery.

- Open the Customize the Quick Access Toolbar window, select a button, and click the Remove button. Right-click the Quick Access toolbar and choose Customize Quick Access Toolbar to open the window.

- Change the order of buttons: Open the Customize the Quick Access Toolbar window, select a button, and click the Move Up or Move Down button. To open this window, right-click the Quick Access toolbar and choose Customize the Quick Access Toolbar.

- Move the toolbar below the ribbon: Right-click the Quick Access toolbar and choose Show Quick Access Toolbar Below the Ribbon on the shortcut menu. To return the Quick Access toolbar to the top of the screen, right-click the toolbar and choose Show Quick Access Toolbar Above the Ribbon.

- Reset the Quick Access toolbar: Right-click the Quick Access toolbar and choose Customize Quick Access Toolbar to open the Customize the Quick Access Toolbar window. Then click the Reset button and choose Reset Only Quick Access Toolbar on the gallery.

Add and Remove Quick Access Toolbar Buttons

① Click the Home tab.

② Right-click the Text Highlight Color button and choose Add to Quick Access toolbar to add this button to the toolbar.

③ Click the Customize Quick Access Toolbar button.

④ Select Redo on the gallery to add the Undo button to the toolbar.

⑤ Right-click the Quick Access toolbar and choose Customize Quick Access Toolbar to open the OneNote Options dialog box to the Customize the Quick Access Toolbar window.

⑥ On the left side of the window, select the Cut button.

⑦ Click Add to add the Cut button to the Quick Access toolbar.

⑧ Click OK.

(continued on next page)

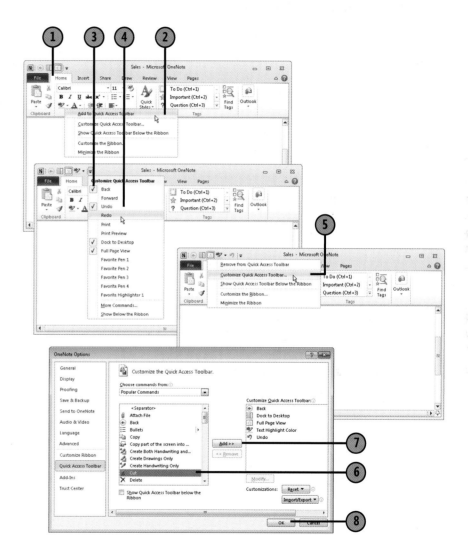

Add and Remove Quick Access
Toolbar Buttons *(continued)*

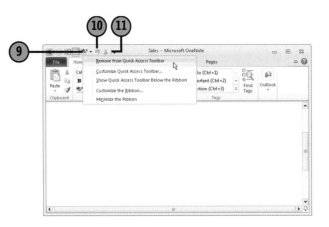

9 Right-click the Text Highlight Color button on the Quick Access toolbar and choose Remove from Quick Access Toolbar.

10 Right-click the Undo button and choose Remove from Quick Access Toolbar.

11 Right-click the Cut button and choose Remove from Quick Access toolbar.

See Also

"Reset Quick Access Toolbar Customizations" on page 205 to learn how to reset the toolbar to its default settings.

Change the Order of Buttons on the Quick Access Toolbar

(1) Click the Customize Quick Access Toolbar button.

(2) Choose More Commands on the gallery to open the Customize the Quick Access Toolbar window.

(3) On the right side of the screen, select the Full Page View button.

(4) Click the Move Up button.

(5) Click OK.

Reposition the Quick Access Toolbar

1. Right-click the Quick Access Toolbar and choose Show Quick Access Toolbar Below the Ribbon.

2. Right-click the Quick Access toolbar and choose Show Quick Access Toolbar Above the Ribbon.

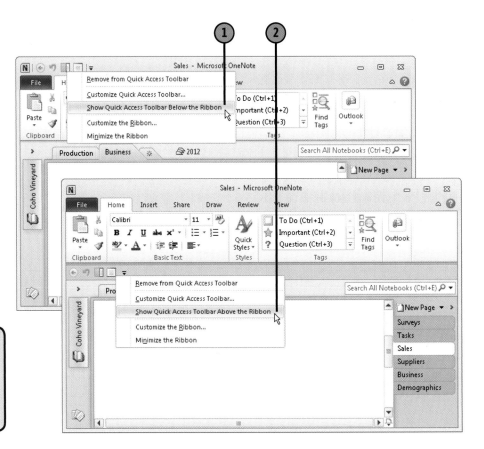

Tip

You can also reposition the Quick Access toolbar by clicking the Customize Quick Access Toolbar button. On the shortcut menu, choose Show Below the Ribbon or Show Above the Ribbon.

Reset Quick Access Toolbar Customizations

(1) Right-click the Quick Access toolbar and chose Customize Quick Access Toolbar.

(2) Click Reset and choose Reset Only Quick Access Toolbar on the gallery.

(3) Click Yes in the Are You Sure? message box.

(4) Click OK.

Customizing the Ribbon

The ribbon is the stretch of ground across the top of the One-Note screen. It is composed of different tabs; on each tab are commands divided into groups. To undertake a task, you click a tab on the ribbon, look for the group with the commands you need, and choose commands.

To get more out of OneNote, you can customize the ribbon. You can create your own tabs, and within those tabs, your own groups; and you can populate these custom groups with commands of your choice. Moreover, you can rename tabs and groups; change the order of tabs on the ribbon; and within each tab, change the order of command groups.

Opening the Customize the Ribbon Window

To customize the ribbon, start by opening the Customize the Ribbon window in the OneNote Options dialog box. Use one of these techniques to open this window:

- Click File and choose Options. Then, in the OneNote Options dialog box, click Customize Ribbon.

- Right-click a tab name on the ribbon and choose Customize the Ribbon on the shortcut menu.

About the Customize the Ribbon Window

The left side of the Customize the Ribbon window lists all One-Note commands. To add commands to the ribbon, start by selecting the command you want to add on the left side of the window. To locate and select a command, choose a subset of commands on the Choose Commands From menu (or choose All Commands) and then click the command's name.

The right side of the Customize the Ribbon window shows the names of tabs; and within each tab, the names of groups; and within each group, the names of commands currently on the ribbon. To display the names of tabs, groups, and commands within groups, click Expand buttons next to tab names and group names.

Techniques for Customizing the Ribbon

Use these techniques in the Customize the Ribbon window to customize the ribbon:

- Create a new tab: On the right side of the window, select the tab you want your new tab to follow. Then click the New Tab button. OneNote creates a new tab and new group for the tab. Select the new tab (it's called "New Tab [Custom]"), click the Rename button, and enter a name for the tab. (Do the same for the new group that OneNote created.)

- Remove a tab: Select the tab and click the Remove button. You can only remove tabs you created yourself.

- Create a group within a tab: On the right side of the window, select the group that you want your new group to follow. Then click the New Group button. OneNote creates a group called "New Group (Custom)." Click the Rename button and enter a name for the group.

- Remove a group: On the right side of the window, right-click the group you want to remove and choose Remove. You can only remove groups you created.

- Add commands to tabs: On the left side of the window, select the command you want to add. On the right side of the window, select a custom group where you want the command to be. Then click the Add button. Commands can be added only to custom groups.

- Remove commands from tabs: On the right side of the window, select the command you want to remove. Then click the Remove button. Commands can be removed only from custom groups.

- Rename tabs and groups: On the right side of the window, select the tab or group, and click the Rename button. Then enter a name in the Rename dialog box and click OK.

- Relocate tabs on the ribbon and groups within a tab: On the right side of the window, select the tab or group. Then click Move Up or Move Down as many times as necessary to move the tab or group where you want it to be.

- Reset your ribbon customizations: To undo customizations, use one of these techniques in the Customize the Ribbon window:

  - Restore a tab: Right-click the tab and choose Reset tab (or select the tab, click the Reset button, and choose Reset Only Selected Ribbon Tab on the gallery).

  - Restore all customizations: Click the Reset button and choose Reset All Customizations on the gallery.

Create and Remove a Tab

1. Right-click any tab name on the Ribbon and choose Customize the Ribbon on the shortcut menu.

2. Under Customize the Ribbon, select the tab that your new tab will follow.

3. Click the New Tab button.

4. Select the tab you created (it's called New Tab [Custom]).

5. Click the Rename button.

6. Enter a name in the Rename dialog box and click OK.

7. Select the tab you created and named.

8. Click the Remove button (you can remove only tabs you created).

9. Click OK.

Create and Remove a Group in a Tab

1. Right-click any tab name on the ribbon and choose Customize the Ribbon on the shortcut menu.

2. Under Customize the Ribbon, click the Expand button next to the tab that the new group will go in.

3. Select the group that your new group will follow.

4. Click the New Group button.

5. Click the Rename button.

6. In the Rename dialog box, choose a symbol for the group, enter a name, and click OK.

7. Select the group you created and named.

8. Click the Remove button (you can remove only groups you created).

9. Click OK.

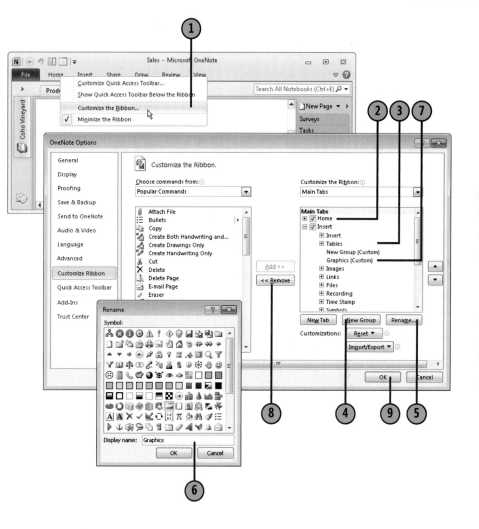

Rename a Tab and Group

1. Right-click any tab name on the ribbon and choose Customize the Ribbon on the shortcut menu.

2. Under Customize the Ribbon on the right side of the window, select a tab you want to rename.

3. Click the Rename button.

4. Enter a name and click OK.

5. Click the Expand button next to a tab name to expose the names of its groups.

6. Select the group you want to rename.

7. Click the Rename button.

8. Enter a name and click OK.

9. Click OK to close the OneNote Options dialog box.

Relocate a Tab and Group

1. Click File.

2. Choose Options.

3. Select Customize Ribbon.

4. Select the tab you want to relocate.

5. Click Move Up or Move Down.

6. Click the Expand button next to a tab name to expose the names of its groups.

7. Select a group you want to relocate on a tab.

8. Click Move Up or Move Down.

9. Click OK to close the OneNote Options dialog box.

Add Commands to and Remove Commands from Custom groups

① Right-click any tab name on the ribbon and choose Customize the Ribbon on the shortcut menu.

② Under Choose Commands From, select a command (if you have trouble finding a command, open the menu and choose a subset of commands).

③ Under Customize the Ribbon, click the Expand button next to a tab to see its command groups.

④ Select the name of a custom group that you created.

⑤ Click Add.

⑥ Select a command that you want to remove (it must be in a custom group).

⑦ Click Remove.

⑧ Click OK.

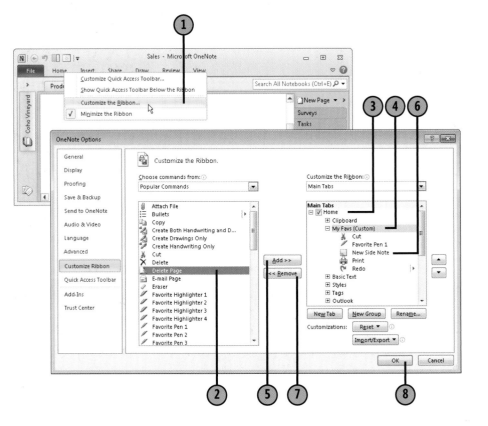

Try This!

Select a command and click Move Up or Move Down to position it in a group.

Reset Your Ribbon Customizations

1. Click File.

2. Choose Options.

3. Select the Customize Ribbon category.

4. Click the Reset button.

5. Choose Reset All Customizations.

6. Click Yes in the Delete dialog box.

7. Click OK.

Tip ✓

You can also reset only the customizations you made to a particular tab on the ribbon. Select a tab name on the right side of the Customize the Ribbon window, click the Reset button, and choose Reset Only Selected Ribbon tab (or right-click the tab name and choose Reset Tab).

20

Using OneNote Web App

Anyone can use OneNote Web App, the online version of Microsoft OneNote 2010. You don't have to pay a fee or even install Microsoft Office 2010 on your computer. All you need is an Internet connection and an account with Windows Live.

OneNote Web App is an abridged version of OneNote 2010. It doesn't offer as many commands, but it does offer an excellent opportunity to coauthor notebooks with others. Because the notebooks are kept online at Windows Live, not on someone's computer, anyone with an Internet connection and a Windows Live account can access the notebooks. Hundreds of people can coauthor a single notebook. What's more, they can work on a notebook at the same time, and if they need a command that isn't in OneNote Web App, they can open the file in OneNote and edit it there.

Introducing Web Applications

OneNote Web App is a *web application*, also called an *online application*. Web applications work a little differently from other applications. Instead of running from software that is installed on a computer, they run from software on a web server on the Internet. To run a web application, you open your web browser, go to the website where the web application is, start the web application, and give commands through your browser to the web application.

What's the advantage of doing that? For one thing, you don't have to install any software on your computer. And you don't have to update the software, either, because technicians on the web server do that. Web application software—One-Note Web App included—is always up to date.

Another advantage of web applications such as One-Note Web App is this: You can store your files on a web server where you can always get them and where others can work on them too. Web applications permit many people to work on the same file. OneNote Web App is especially good in this regard. A person running OneNote 2010 and another running OneNote Web App can coauthor the same notebook at the same time.

OneNote Web App is one of four web applications in the OfficeO Web Apps. The others are Word Web App, Excel Web App, and PowerPoint Web App.

Getting Ready to Use OneNote Web App

OneNote Web App is the online version of OneNote. On its Home, Insert, and View tab, OneNote Web App offers many, but not all, of the commands in OneNote. However, if you can't find the command you need in OneNote Web App, you can open your notebook in OneNote, work on it there, and save it to the Internet folder where your notebook is stored.

Office Web App software and notebooks you share using OneNote Web App are stored on Windows Live, a Microsoft website that offers web-based applications and services. On one of these services, called SkyDrive, you can store and share OneNote notebooks.

Signing Up for Windows Live

Sign up for Windows Live at this web page: *http://home.live.com*. If you want to share notebooks, get a Hotmail account when you sign up. You can use your Hotmail account to send invitations to others to share your notebooks.

Go to *http://home.live.com* to sign in to Windows Live. To sign out, click the Sign Out link in the upper-right corner of the Windows Live window.

See Also

"Using OneNote Web App in Office 365" on page 225 to learn how to use OneNote Web App in Office 365.

Tip

OneNote Web App is also available to businesses and organizations that subscribe to Office 365. The features are nearly identical to those in Windows Live.

Home tab

Insert tab

View tab

Notebook open in
OneNote 2010

Creating SkyDrive Folders for Storing Notebooks

On Windows Live, files are kept in SkyDrive folders. SkyDrive is where you create OneNote notebooks, create and manage folders for storing notebooks, and invite other people to collaborate with you.

Click SkyDrive on the Windows Live taskbar to open SkyDrive. Then, on the Create taskbar, click the Create Folder button to create a folder. After you enter a name for your folder, be sure to click the Change link and choose a Share With setting if you intend to coauthor notebooks with others:

- **Everyone (Public):** Windows Live friends and guests whom you invite to the folder can see notebooks but not edit them.

- **My Friends and Their Friends:** Your Windows Live friends and friends you have in common with your Windows Live friends can access the folder.

- **Friends:** All your Windows Live friends, including your limited-access friends, can access the folder.

- **Some Friends:** Your Windows Live friends, except friends with limited access, can access the folder.

- **Me:** The folder is private, and only you can open it.

For more information about SkyDrive, go to this web page: *http://explore.live.com/windows-live-skydrive-help-center.*

Creating a Notebook

Starting in SkyDrive (click SkyDrive on the Windows Live taskbar), use one of these techniques to create a notebook:

- Click the OneNote Notebook icon on the Create taskbar.

- Click SkyDrive on the Windows Live taskbar and choose New OneNote notebook.

Then enter a name for the notebook and click the Save button. If you intend to share the notebook, click the Change link and choose a Share With setting.

Click the File button and choose Close to close a notebook. To open a notebook, open the SkyDrive folder in which the notebook is stored and then click the notebook's name.

Create a Notebook

① Click the OneNote Notebook icon.

② Enter a name.

③ Click Save.

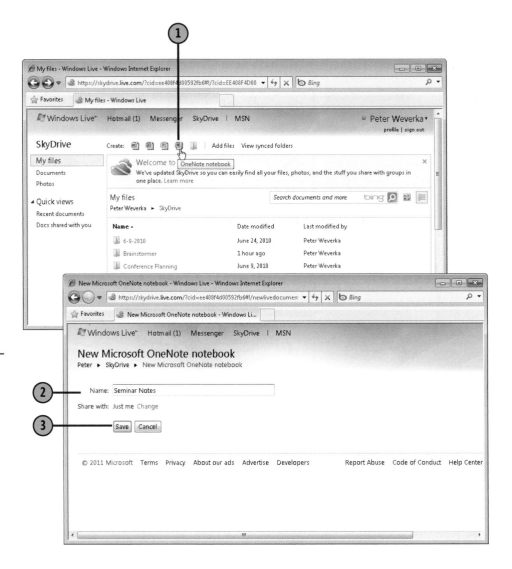

Exploring OneNote Web App

OneNote Web App is an abridged version of OneNote 2010. If you are familiar with OneNote 2010, OneNote Web App looks familiar.

Unlike OneNote 2010, the Navigation bar in OneNote Web App lists only section and page names. Click a page name to open a different page. Click section names to expand and collapse sections.

To write a note, double-click on the screen and start typing.

Instead of six tabs on the ribbon, OneNote Web App has three tabs:

- Home: Offers commands for formatting text, tagging notes, and spell checking.

- Insert: Offers commands for creating new pages and sections, creating a table, inserting pictures and clip art, and creating hyperlinks.

- View: Offers commands for changing views, showing who wrote notes, and seeing different versions of a page.

Go to the Insert tab to create a new page or section (you can also click the New Page button on the Navigation bar to create a page).

Explore OneNote Web App

1. Click the Home tab.

2. Click the View tab.

3. Click Reading View.

4. Click Edit in Browser to return to Editing View.

5. Click the Insert tab.

6. Click the New Page button.

7. Enter a page name.

8. Double-click on the screen and type a note.

Tip

To rename a page or section, right-click the name of the page or section and choose New Page or New Section. Then enter a new name.

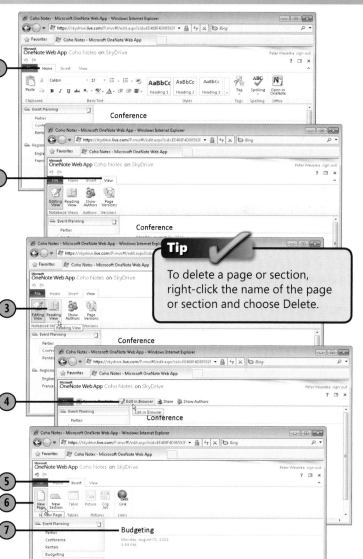

Tip

To delete a page or section, right-click the name of the page or section and choose Delete.

Opening a Notebook in OneNote 2010

When you want to do a task that you can do in OneNote 2010 but not OneNote Web App, open your notebook in OneNote 2010. Starting in OneNote Web App, you open a notebook in OneNote 2010 with one of these techniques:

- On the Home tab, click the Open in OneNote button.

- Click File and choose Open in OneNote.

- On the View tab, click Reading View, and then click the Open in OneNote button.

You can tell when you've opened a notebook that is stored at Windows Live because the Sync (synchronization) Status icon appears beside the notebook's name in the Navigation bar. If a check mark appears beside the icon, the OneNote 2010 and OneNote Web App edition of the file are in sync with one another. You can right-click the icon and choose Sync This Notebook Now (or press Shift+F9) to synchronize the notebooks. Right-click and choose Notebook Sync Status to find out when the notebooks were last synchronized.

Open a Notebook in OneNote 2010

(1) Click the Home tab.

(2) Click Open in OneNote.

(3) In OneNote 2010, write a note and notice that the check mark disappears from the Sync Status icon (it disappears because the local and online notebooks are out of sync).

(4) Right-click the Sync Status icon and choose Sync This Notebook Now.

See Also

"Sharing a Notebook" on page 192 to learn how to open a notebook, starting in OneNote 2010, on OneNote Web App at Windows Live.

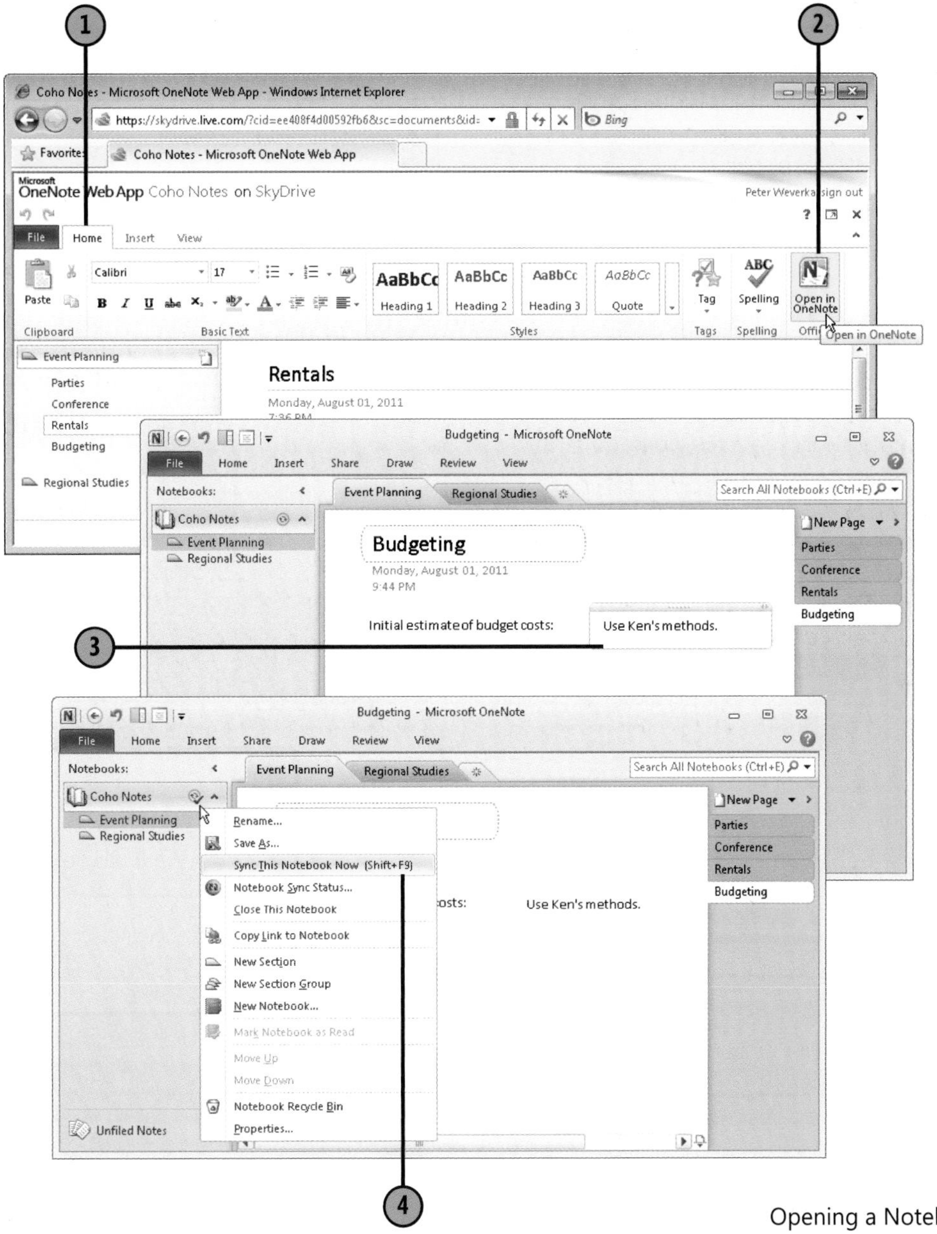
1
2
3
4
Coho Notes - Microsoft OneNote Web App - Windows Internet Explorer
OneNote Web App Coho Notes on SkyDrive
File
Home
Insert
View
Open in OneNote
Rentals
Budgeting - Microsoft OneNote
Budgeting
Initial estimate of budget costs:
Use Ken's methods.
Rename...
Save As...
Sync This Notebook Now (Shift+F9)
Notebook Sync Status...
Close This Notebook
Copy Link to Notebook
New Section
New Section Group
New Notebook...
Mark Notebook as Read
Move Up
Move Down
Notebook Recycle Bin
Properties...

Inviting Others to Coauthor a Notebook

Windows Live offers three techniques for inviting others to coauthor a notebook. With all three techniques, others must be enrolled in Windows Live to edit the notebook.

- Share the SkyDrive folder in which the notebook is located with your friends on Windows Live. Friends can open your public or shared folder and then open the notebook.

- Send out email invitations to visit the folder where the notebook is located. In the public or shared folder on SkyDrive, click Send a Link (this link is located on the right side of the screen). Then, in the Send a Link window, enter an email address, enter a message, and click Send. The recipient can click the View Folder button in the email message to access the folder where the notebook is located.

- Post a hyperlink to the folder where the notebook is located. In the public or shared folder on SkyDrive, click Get a Link. Then, in the Get a Link window, click Copy to copy the folder's URL to the Clipboard. You can paste this URL in a document or web page.

Send an Email Invitation to Coauthor a Notebook

① Open the SkyDrive folder with the notebook you want to coauthor.

② Click Send a Link.

③ Enter the recipient's email address.

④ Write a note to accompany the invitation.

⑤ Select the Require Recipients to Sign in With Windows Live check box. (Recipients must sign in to edit the notebook.)

⑥ Click Send.

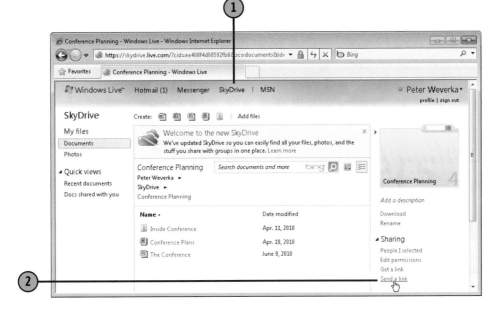

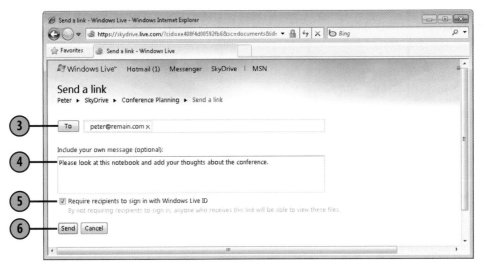

Finding Out Who Wrote Notes

Any number of people can coauthor a notebook on Windows Live. What's more, they can write notes at the same time. And some of them can be working in OneNote Web App and others in OneNote 2010.

When several people coauthor a notebook, how can you tell who wrote which note? Go to the View tab and click the Show Authors button. The names of authors appear beside notes.

Find Out Who Wrote Notes

1 Click the View tab.

2 Click the Show Authors button.

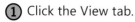

Using OneNote Web App in Office 365

Microsoft Office 365 is a subscription service from Microsoft that permits you to store files on the Internet and collaborate with others using Office Web Application software (OneNote Web App included). Users have email capability, can use a calendar, and can keep a Contact list.

To run Office Web App software with Office 365, you open your web browser, go your Office 365 site, and give commands through your browser to operate the software.

Creating a Notebook

To create a notebook, start on the Home page and go to the Teams Site section. Then click the OneNote icon, enter a name for the notebook, and click OK.

Notebooks you create at Office 365 are available automatically for sharing. You don't need to choose an option to share notebooks with others.

Use these techniques to open and close notebooks:

- Open a notebook: On the main Office 365 page, click Shared Documents and then click the notebook's name.

- Close a notebook: Click the File button and choose Close.

Create a Notebook

1. Go to the Home page.
2. Click the OneNote Icon.
3. Enter a name for the notebook.
4. Click OK.

Exploring OneNote Web App in Office 365

OneNote Web App in Office 365 doesn't offer all the commands found in OneNote 2010. Nevertheless, if you need a favorite command from OneNote 2010, you can open your notebook in OneNote 2010 starting in the OneNote Web App.

To write a note, double-click on the screen and start typing.

OneNote Web App offers three tabs on the ribbon: Home, Insert, and View. Create a new page or section starting on the Insert tab (or click the New Page button on the Navigation bar to create a page).

Starting in OneNote Web App in Office 365, open a notebook in OneNote 2010 with one of these techniques:

- On the Home tab, click the Open in OneNote button.

- Click File and choose Open in OneNote.

- On the View tab, click Reading View and then click the Open in OneNote button.

Index

Symbols

Hotmail account, sharing notebooks
using, 216
hyperlinks for inviting others to coauthor
notebooks, 222–223

I

Ignore button, 109
ignoring word options in spell check, 108,
110
images
formats for, 68
placing in notes, 68
resizing scanned, 67
Ink to Math button, 71
Ink to Text button, 61
Insert buttons
for table rows and columns, 77
inserting
columns (tables), 77
content from scanner or digital camera,
67
file printout, 66
table rows and columns, 77
inserting space between notes, 46
Insert Picture from Scanner or Camera
dialog box, 67–68
Insert Shapes gallery, 120, 121
Insert Space button, 47–48, 123
Insert tab
Attach File button, 65
Equation button, 70
File Printout button, 65, 66
Insert Space button, 47–48
Link button, 88
Picture button, 68
recording menu, 72
Scanner Printout button, 65, 67

Screen Clipping button, 69
Table button, 76
Time-stamping menu, 64
Internet
addresses in spell check, 110
researching topics on, 167
Internet Explorer browser
OneNote save as option, 176
opening linked notes in, 93
Italic text, 52

K

Keep on Top button, 104–105
Keep Source Formatting pasting option,
50
Keep Text Only, pasting option, 50
keyboard shortcuts
aligning table cells, 82
applying heading styles, 54
applying Normal style, 54
Bold, 52
closing Search Results list, 146
converting Unicode character code to
characters, 48
Copying text, 50
Create a New Section, 28
creating side notes, 58
creating subpages, 34–35
Cutting text, 50
date- and time-stamps, 64
displaying ribbon, 7
docking OneNote on side of screen, 11
Find on This Page, 146
Font, 52
Font Color, 52
Font Size, 52
hiding and displaying ribbon, 7

inserting table rows and columns, 77
Italic, 52
left-align paragraphs, 45
linking, 85
Mark As Unread, 194
minimizing and expanding ribbon,
98–99
Move or Copy, 157
moving paragraphs up or down, 50
narrow page tabs, 96
Next Match, 146
Normal view, 147
Numbering button, 63
opening another OneNote window, 104
opening Move or Copy Pages dialog
box, 133
opening Open Notebook dialog box, 21
opening Print dialog box, 174
opening Styles menu, 54
Open Search Results Pane, 149
Pasting text, 50
Previous Match, 146
Promote Subpage, 34–35
Screen Clipping, 69
selecting
all notes on page, 47
multiple files, 65
words in sentence, 49
Strikethrough, 52
Subscript/Superscript, 52
tagging notes, 136
Text Highlight Color, 52
underlining text, 52
undo copy, 133
widening page tabs, 96
zooming in and out, 106